LOAN OFFICERS WANTED

ARSALAN SAADATI

LOAN OFFICERS WANTED

ARSALAN SAADATI

For my beautiful wife who makes everything
worthwhile and to the most amazing mother in the world,
and for my grandmother and grandfather who I can't wait
to see again one day.

Acknowledgements

I want to thank my dearest friends the Chrun family and the Le family for the advice they have all given me throughout the years. I value our friendships more than you know. Thanks especially to Alison for helping me when I really needed it.

To my editor Salvatore Folisi, thank you so much for everything you have done. You have been absolutely amazing throughout the process and I couldn't be any happier with the way everything turned out.

I wouldn't have been able to write this novel if I hadn't worked in the mortgage industry for many years and gone through the experiences that I did. I want to thank all of the people I worked with throughout my career for the memories they gave me. Without them, this wouldn't be possible.

A special thanks to two of the most wonderful women in my life, my mother and my wife. Thanks mom for always being there for me and showing me your love. To my wife, thank you for never giving up on us and for making me a better man.

LOAN OFFICERS WANTED

~ ONE ~

ANTHONY COUSTO WALKED OUT of his office into the hot summer sun. The streets were busy and vibrant with cars speeding their drivers to important midday appointments. Stepping onto the sidewalk, he caught the glimmer of the high noon sun reflecting off the silver lines in his royal blue suit. It gave him a sense of importance and belonging amidst the many businesses surrounding his own. Turning left onto the sidewalk with his gaze set towards the nearby park, Anthony felt the relief of the expansive air which filled his lungs with the familiar scent of nature mixed with industry. He needed a moment, alone, to reflect on this point to which his life had arrived, and all he'd done to get there. And the park provided a regular respite from the sometimes agonizing drone of his office. As he walked towards the park, he wondered how making so much money could make so much trouble in his life. How something that appeared to be so good, could end up being so bad.

Crossing the street, Anthony almost stopped to cuss out the ignorant driver who barely stopped in time at the crosswalk. However, his mind was so occupied, so filled with a tremendous tumult of emotion and questions hovering over his life like the shadows of unseen ghosts, that he didn't have time for such trivialities. No, this day, he needed to think about his life and how he was living it. Although he had reached a pinnacle of material success that most people would never know, today Anthony Cousto was fraught with a burgeoning realization that this so-called success was nothing more than a glorified stage-set he had built around himself. And today, it was all beginning to crumble.

As he walked through the park, the trees provided some intermittent shelter from the radiant sun which was somehow incongruous with the multiple layers of his suit. However, beneath the sun and the sporadic shade and all the layers of his finely tailored royal blue suit, on this 90-something degree day in Southern California, Anthony Cousto was sweating. It was not just the heat of the day that created this rise in his body temperature. It was the slow burn of his life. It was the recognition of the unrecognizable person he had become in order to make money. Distorted, deformed, and camouflaged to kill in the name of Capitalism. Anthony was no longer in possession of his own soul or destiny. He had gone askew, departed from himself upon a path of gross deviation on which he had become a nearly sociopathic and delusional aberration of his original and authentic person.

Anthony slowly wound his way through the park, with its green grass and cool ponds, knowing that it too was a fabrication, that without the extensive manipulations of irrigation this park would be naught but a dried expanse of desert scrub. He wanted to know what was true in his life, but Anthony knew it had nothing to do with the contents of the envelope he held in his hands. He was beginning to see that all the money in the world couldn't make him well, nor could it grant him a real and lasting happiness. At last, sitting on the park bench, Anthony's fingers rubbed slowly back and forth on the paper of the envelope, as if to remind him that it was real. Although he had worked very intensely to attain it, he felt ashamed and undeserving for having earned so much money at other people's expense. He glanced around himself as if to notice if anyone was looking. Then, slowly he edged the tip of his finger beneath the end flap of the envelope and tore it open, whereupon he gradually lifted out a check from Fairtex Mortgage paid to himself, Anthony Cousto, in the amount of $280,000.

I knew I would always be rich, Anthony thought to himself. *But I never knew the price I would have to pay to get there. I just made $280,000 for closing 40 loans in 30 days. And the craziest part of it all is I'm only 26 years old.*

~ TWO ~

WHEN ANTHONY WAS A CHILD his parents were hard-working folks who struggled day-in and day-out just to keep up with the bills. Anthony's dad, Michael, drove a taxi cab seven days a week to provide for his family, while his mom, Elizabeth, ran the house. At six feet tall and rather stocky, his dad was a foreboding figure to Anthony. Although his sparkling green eyes revealed something of the inner goodness and warmth that Michael felt towards his son. As a child, Anthony thought his dad was the hardest working guy in the whole world because he was always working. He didn't understand how his dad could work so hard, so much of the time, and they could still be so poor. This didn't seem fair at all to Anthony.

Anthony's mom was an attractive woman with a slender figure. She had cheerful blonde hair, and her gentle brown eyes were comforting to Anthony whenever he became upset. Although she stayed at home, Anthony's mom didn't work any less than his dad. From morning until night she was busy taking care of Anthony and his sister, cooking the meals, cleaning the house, and running errands. After all this, she somehow managed to put up with the bickering and complaining from Anthony's dad. Usually it was about stupid things that didn't really amount to much. But, in the end, it all came down to the bills and the lack of money to pay them.

Anthony's parents fought all the time. He remembers his father stomping around the living room holding a fistful of bills, waving them angrily at his mother. "How the hell are we gonna pay this bill with all the god damn things you buy!" his dad shouted. Although his mom didn't like to argue, and generally displayed and caring and considerate demeanor, on such occasions she yelled right back at his dad. "I don't know, maybe you should stop going to the casino on the way home from work every day and pissing away your money on gambling!"

On this particular occasion, Anthony sat with his little sister Maria at the top of the stairs, holding his hands over her ears so that she wouldn't hear their parents yelling at each other. But this never really worked. His sister could hear them perfectly as she cried under her breath, trying to understand why her parents were so angry. But Anthony knew why. It was always about the money. His dad complained about it almost every day. Why did Anthony's mom buy such expensive clothes? Why didn't she buy the cheaper brands? Why did the money always seem to run out so fast? Why was there never enough to pay for everything? Anthony heard his dad complain about the money until he thought he would throw up. Although he appreciated how hard his dad worked, he didn't like the way he yelled at his mom, and he really didn't like the nightly arguments.

The day after this argument, Anthony stood outside his school waiting for the bus. Suddenly, his dad pulled up in the cab. He rolled down the passenger window, and said, "Get in! I'll take you home today, Anthony." Stepping into the car and sitting down on the seat, Anthony could smell the familiar burnt odor of his dad's cigarettes. Once Anthony was inside the car, his father drove and was quiet for a short while before breaking the silence.

"How are you son?"

"I'm okay," Anthony replied.

"How's school going? You have your eye on any girls?"

"School's okay. But I don't really want any girls."

"What do you mean, you don't want any girls?" Anthony's dad replied with an inquisitive tone of disbelief. "I remember when I was your age. I didn't have just one girl; I had lots of girls, and they were all fighting over me!"

Anthony squirmed a little in his seat, feeling uncomfortable talking about girls and trying to explain why he wasn't all that interested in them.

"Dad," Anthony began slowly, "it's not that girls don't like me. Or even that I don't like them. It's just that I see how you and mom fight all the time, and it seems like you guys are never happy. So why would I want that?"

Anthony's dad took a deep breath and gazed down briefly at the floor of the cab. He felt a bit stunned by what his son had said and took a moment to reflect. Then, abruptly, almost instinctively, he pulled the car over to the side of the road by a gas station and parked. As the car keys jingled, hanging from the ignition, he looked at his son and searched for the right words to say to him.

"To be honest with you Anthony, the reason I picked you up from school today is that I wanted to talk with you about the fight me and your mom had last night."

His dad looked out the window at the short green field of spring grass and the residential houses lined up at its far end. Anthony looked at his dad and saw that he was thinking hard about what to say to him.

"Anthony, your mother and I love each other more than anything in the world. She is my angel, and I adore her more than my own life."

"So then why do you guys fight so much?" Anthony replied.

"Let me explain something to you son," Anthony's dad began. "I never went to high school or even dreamed of going to college. Your grandfather pulled me out of school so that I could help him with the family business. Then your mom and I married early, and she got pregnant. So, we made the family our first priority, and neither one of us got a college education. When the family business closed down, I didn't have many options for work and got involved in some shady business that could have led to trouble."

Anthony's dad paused to take a breath and put his fingers to his forehead, squinting his eyes together in an effort to collect his thoughts.

"But I had to put food on the table for you and your mom and your sister, and I couldn't do that very well from behind prison bars. So I left all that bad business behind, and we moved out of Boston to find a better life here in Irvine." As his dad talked, Anthony wondered about what kind of bad things his dad could have done. He couldn't really imagine any other than maybe just yelling at people, because he had always known his dad as a very good-hearted person. "I wanted to see you and your sister grow up in a safe neighborhood," his father continued. "And I wanted you to have some pride in your father. I know driving a cab isn't the most glamorous job in the world, but it's the only way I know how to try to provide you with the opportunities in life that I never had. Unfortunately, all those opportunities that I want for you and your sister cost a lot of money."

At this, Anthony began to feel a bit restless. He knew everything cost money and that there was never enough because he had heard his parents fighting about it almost every night. But he respected his dad. And he appreciated his honesty. So he focused with every ounce of concentration he had to keep listening. However, what his dad said next really got his attention.

"Your mother and I don't fight because we don't love each other Anthony. It's because of money. That's why you need to finish high school and go to college, so you can get a good job that pays a lot of money. Then you won't have the problems that I do."

Anthony's dad paused to let everything he had said sink in and make sense to his son. Then he finished his story by saying "So, do you understand now, son, why your education is so important?"

Anthony nodded his head, saying "Yeah dad, I do."

Then, just as quickly as he had pulled the car over to the side of the road, Anthony's father turned the key in the ignition and drove it back onto the road and onward to their home. That was the first time Anthony's dad had ever opened up to him, and he knew what his dad said had to be true. That day, Anthony realized he had to be rich when he grew up, and he knew he was willing to do whatever it took.

~ THREE ~

At 22 YEARS OLD, Anthony had become a confident, well-spoken young man. He was tall and good-looking and had always attracted the ladies with his charming smile and penetrating green eyes. Although he was the kind of guy that young women loved to bring home to meet their parents, there was something daring and risky about Anthony that gave the girls a sense of dangerous adventure that most of them couldn't resist. Although they all said that they wanted a nice guy, Anthony knew that in secret the girls really wanted a bad boy who would give them a thrill. And he had always been up for the challenge. Until he met his match in Kelly and fell completely.

Although the wild rampages of his early romances had been nothing short of titillating, Anthony had found a more long-lasting and fulfilling relationship with Kelly that also carried an underside of cryptic intensity and enthralling sexual passion. So much so that he and Kelly had been inspired to get married. The regularity of his relationship with Kelly gave Anthony the sensible groundwork to become a moderately good student. And so he had plodded along with diligence upon the path to attaining his college degree and was now at the threshold of his commencement.

On the day of his college graduation, Anthony stood nervously on the side of the stage. He had worked very hard to get this far. He had made his parents proud and he felt a sense of great accomplishment. Waiting for his name to be called, Anthony looked down at his flowing black gown and his shiny black shoes. He had polished them just this morning in anticipation of his graduation. He had always taken pride in how he appeared to others, but on this day he was proud about more than just looking good, he was proud that he had applied himself to a rigorous four years of college education and had proven himself worthy of coming out the other side as a graduate.

Everyone Anthony loved was in the crowd waiting to see him walk across the stage. His parents, his wife, his family and friends. He felt happy that he could demonstrate his academic attainment to them. As he waited in line, he glanced around at the other graduates, some of them had become close friends over the previous four years. He could see from their smiling faces that they too felt a sense of exaltation at having arrived at this day. The wind blew a fresh spring air upon his face, and now that he was to receive his diploma, he could feel the summoning of a great change coming into his life—though he did not know where it came from or what it had in store for him.

As the person in front of him walked across the stage, Anthony felt the electricity building in his body as he knew his own moment of recognition was coming next. On the verge of receiving the greatest public award he had ever known, Anthony reflected on how happy he had made his parents by attending and graduating from college. That alone, had made it all worthwhile to him.

"Anthony Cousto!"

The voice calling his name boomed through the loudspeakers, snapping Anthony out of his reverie, whereupon he walked forthright across the stage in front of the huge crowd of nearly a thousand observers. Stepping up to the podium, the familiar professor who had been one of Anthony's favorites smiled at him.

"Congratulations Anthony!" he said, and handed Anthony his college diploma, wishing him the best of luck in the future.

After nodding and thanking his professor, Anthony took a moment to look into the crowd, seeing so many unfamiliar faces but knowing that the ones he loved were there somewhere mixed in with all the others. The sun was bright and, combined with the quick glory of the moment, seemed to almost blind him. Holding tightly onto his diploma he preceded across the stage with a feeling of relief, like a hiker in the wilderness who has forded a rumbling river, towards the others who had already walked.

When everyone's name had been called and all had received their diplomas, there was a great moment of celebration with many of the graduates tossing their caps high into the midday air. Anthony left his cap on his head, but cheered vociferously with the rest of his graduating class. Then he stood up to find his family. Walking through the crowd, he hugged and congratulated many of the graduates who he knew.

As he wished a fellow graduate well, suddenly his parents appeared before him. His mother rushed to give him a hug, exclaiming, "I'm so proud of you Anthony!" She was crying and had a look of adoration for her son in her eyes.

His father was there too. He beamed upon Anthony, saying "Son you made me very proud today. You're the only family member to ever graduate college." His father hugged Anthony, and spoke secretly into his ear, "I know this is only the beginning of all the good things you will do in life."

"Thanks dad!" Anthony replied with a grin after hugging his father. "I always wanted to make you proud of me."

"You did son. You did," Anthony's dad replied.

His wife Kelly had stood in the background to allow Anthony's parents congratulate him first, but as soon as she saw that they were done she immediately came and encircled him with a warm and loving embrace. Looking directly into his eyes, she said "Congratulations, you made it! I love you so much."

With blonde hair and striking green eyes, Kelly was a beautiful woman, and Anthony knew he was lucky to have found her. They had been married for two years and Anthony felt that she was his ideal woman. The perfect match of beauty and brains, Kelly was both sexually stimulating and intellectually adept. She also had a good heart and encouraged Anthony with his own goals. Having met in a college history class at the beginning of his studies, they had fallen quickly and completely in love. Anthony always thought Kelly was much smarter than him, so sure of herself and able to hold her own in any situation. Although he loved her deeply, he also truly admired her.

They had married a year before her graduation, and her parents who were rather wealthy had arranged a phenomenal wedding celebration for them. After her own graduation, Kelly had landed a job at an upscale accounting firm making sixty thousand dollars a year. Her parents were happy about this and had expected as much as her dad was a big shot lawyer doing class action law suits in San Francisco. Needless to say, they had lots of money. Anthony had always felt they expected him to provide as grand of a lifestyle for their daughter as they had. Although he knew they liked him, he felt an unspoken pressure to get his degree and start to earn a good wage while doing something as impressive as Kelly's father. He wasn't really sure how he would do this, or even if he could. But now that he had graduated, in the back of his mind he was more aware that their expectations for him to succeed would increase.

Anthony kissed his wife and thanked her for being there. Looking around him, he noticed a group of family members in a small circle all waiting for his acknowledgement. His sister Maria was there too. As a grown woman she had filled out exceptionally well and was both curvaceous and fit. When she was a teenager, Anthony had fought the guys off of her, but by now she'd become independent and he only urged her to be selective with her choice of suitors. She smiled shyly and gave him a hug. "Congratulations Anthony!" she said.

"Thanks sis," Anthony retorted. "I know I'm going to see you walk across a stage like this one day too. Although I think you might look better in this stupid robe than I do!"

"You bet I will!" his sister retorted. Anthony smiled and his sister laughed. They had always had a special closeness and it was good for them to see each other this day. With her similar stature, blonde hair, and brown eyes, Maria had always reminded Anthony of his mother. She had naturally inherited all his mother's graceful mannerisms, wit, and ebullience. And she was quick on her feet to meet Anthony's playfully challenging sarcasm.

Anthony's aunt and uncle from Boston who he hadn't seen for years were there too. Even his best friend Ethan Miller who had graduated a year earlier came to congratulate Anthony on his graduation. About fifteen pounds overweight, Ethan had short black hair and glistening hazel eyes that shot beams of energy around wherever he looked. Ethan was usually on the prowl looking for something to satisfy himself. He had an outgoing, contagious energy that came with a knack for getting into trouble. Although he channeled some of his intensity to working out in the gym, drinking and partying usually got the better of him so he never made much progress with his physique. Ethan made Anthony's family line up around him so he could take their picture. Afterwards, a bunch of Anthony's friends and fellow graduates walked up and all congratulated him.

"Anthony, let's take a picture with you and your friends too!" his mom said, as she swiftly took the camera from Ethan and made all of them squeeze together and say "Cheese!"

Anthony was glad to see his fellow-graduate friends. There was Sam Hillman, who studied engineering and had just accepted a sixty-five-thousand-dollar a year job working out of Sacramento for a huge company. And his friend John Anderson, a black guy who was a marketing major on his way to Law School. Huang Fu, whom we just called "Steve," was an Asian guy with a major in IT. He had just gotten a job doing web design at a high-profile company in San Diego, making about fifty-thousand-dollar a year.

Everyone was laughing and happy as Anthony introduced his friends to his family. It was an occasion for celebration, and Anthony smiled too, feeling a sense of real accomplishment at having completed his studies. But inside himself, he was worried. His friends had all acquired jobs before graduating, but he didn't have the slightest idea what he was going to do next. Having graduated with a 3.0 GPA, he was happy as hell just to be done with it. But so far he'd gone to ten interviews and had no luck with any of them. He had twenty thousand dollars in student loans and fifteen thousand in credit card debt, and had just quit his job working at the Mexican restaurant where he'd put in forty hours a week while attending school full time. He had the drive to succeed, and knew that failure was not an option. He just needed someone to give him an opportunity.

~ **FOUR** ~

$\mathbf{A}$ COUPLE DAYS AFTER the graduation ceremony, Anthony met with his friends Sam, John, and Steve at the basketball court. Throughout college they had come to play basketball as a way of working off stress and having fun. Like most guys, it was also a way they showed off their male bravado, but without being too serious.

"I can't believe this is the last time we're going to be at this gym," Sam said, shaking his head. "Just the four of us shooting around." Sam was Asian and short. He wasn't very good at basketball but enjoyed the exercise and the camaraderie with his friends. He had the typical late 90's short haircut spiked on the top with gel. Sam wore glasses, even on the court, and was a nice, intelligent guy who people liked to talk to. A bit nervous, he didn't want to attempt the first shot so he threw the ball to Steve.

"I know, damn where did the time go?" Steve replied, aiming for the hoop then throwing an awful shot that nearly missed the backboard.

"Well, thank god we aren't going to see Steve play basketball again, 'cause you suck more than anyone I know!" John exclaimed, before making a nice lay-up shot with an ease that made Steve want to cry. Steve was also Asian, a slightly heavy, very dark-skinned Pacific Islander who was a little taller than Sam, but much worse on the court. In fact, Steve was so dark people often thought he was half-black, a fact that amused John to no end. He was the quietest, shyest guy in the pack, and had terrible luck with the ladies. He often complained about how hard it was to get laid, but he didn't do much to change the situation. Hanging out with John and Anthony had occasionally given him the opportunity to enjoy the overflow of available women and to ride on the crest of their wave. But left to his own devices he was a total dud.

Anthony quickly picked up the ball and passed it back to Steve saying, "C'mon dude! You can do better than that first one." However, his overwhelming laughter only made Steve more angry. So he passed the ball back really hard back to Anthony, saying, "Shit man, I don't see you making no dunk shots!"

Anthony caught the ball still laughing and said, "You guys remember when Steve stole the ball and then scored the winning basket on the wrong side?"

At this point everyone on the court started cracking up so hard they were bent over with laughter. Everyone, that is, except Steve.

"What the fuck!" Steve sputtered. "I told you guys I was just nervous."

Never wanting to upset anyone, Sam just avoided eye contact with Steve and motioned for Anthony to take a shot.

Then John added in "Man, Steve I have to admit you're pretty horrible on the court. Anthony's right on this one." John was young and tall and filled with enthusiasm. Although he proclaimed himself to be the best basketball player around, in truth he was average at best. But his attitude carried him through, and from time to time he did make a great shot.

"Maybe if you weren't always hogging the ball like you're god damn Magic Johnson I'd get a little more practice shooting," Steve defended himself, knowing they were all right.

Making a bad shot himself, Anthony stopped laughing and got a serious look on his face. "Let me ask you guys something, did you really learn anything in these last four years?"

"Yeah, I learned a lot," Sam replied quickly, looking a bit confused.

"Really? Like what?" Anthony answered.

"Like how to build a bridge or a building!" Sam exclaimed. "Is that enough?"

John attempted another shot from where he was standing, but barely missed. "Shit Anthony, maybe if you weren't so busy cheating off my tests or having me write your English papers you would have learned something too!" he said, obviously also pissed that he missed the shot.

Now it was Steve's turn to laugh at Anthony. "That's true, you did cheat a lot Anthony," he said, running up to grab the ball and missing a simple shot just two feet away from the hoop.

"What are you guys talking about? I didn't cheat! I mean not all the time." Anthony ran up and grabbed the ball, then dribbled back to the free throw line to make a nice bank shot, as if his anger only increased his shooting skills. "You wrote what, like three pages for me in that class?" he said with obvious consternation, looking at John. "What's the big deal? It's just one friend helping another."

John shook his head and looked at Anthony like he was a stubborn kid making excuses for not doing his chores. "Yeah, but there were only three papers in that class!"

At this, both Steve and Sam busted out with laughter, as Sam tried a hook shot from nearly mid-court and missed by a mile.

"Okay, okay … you got me on that one," Anthony managed to say through his own laughter. "But seriously guys, I learned a little bit about accounting, and that's really it." He paused, holding the basketball in his hands as if his he could divine some elusive answer through its pocked surface. "But how the hell am I going to get a job when no one will even give me a chance? I don't even know what the fuck I want to do! I mean, it's great that I finally graduated. But now what?"

There were a few moments of awkward silence in the gym, as if somehow Anthony had pronounced his own death sentence or told them about some terminal disease he had contracted.

Sam broke the tension, saying "I think you'll do fine Anthony, but just don't get a job that requires a lot of thinking." Before everyone started laughing too hard, Sam quickly qualified his statement, adding "What I mean is, you're more of a sales guy than an intellectual. You're a really good people-person."

"What the hell is that supposed to mean, Sam?" Anthony replied, still feeling the sting of his first comment.

"I think what Sam is trying to say," John broke in, "is that you have a way with words, Anthony. You can convince people to do things they don't want to do. And that's a talent that half the world wished they had!"

"Yeah man," Steve agreed, looking at Anthony, but talking to the other guys. "I hate it when he does that shit to me!"

Everybody laughed, but they all knew that Anthony had the same power over them at times too.

"Okay, that's great that you guys think I'm a smooth talker, but you all have jobs lined up and I don't have shit. And John, you're pretty much set once you get out of Law School. What the fuck am I going to do? I can't rely on Kelly my whole life. Fuck that. I need to get a really good job 'cause I don't want my girl to make more than me."

Running to the corner of the gym to pick up the ball that Sam had recklessly thrown from mid-court, Steve chimed in, "I wouldn't mind if my girl made more than me."

Before Steve could miss another shot, John remarked, "I'm sure you wouldn't Steve, but your problem isn't money. It's actually getting a girl."

All the guys laughed. But then, as if avenging his own unrecognized sexual prowess, Steve actually made a nice jump shot from behind the free throw line that was nothing but net. He felt very pleased with himself and made a mock-smug expression on his face that made everyone laugh even more.

"Didn't you say Ethan wanted to talk to you about work once you get back home?" John said, pouncing on the ball and passing it to Anthony.

"Yeah, but Ethan hasn't had any luck with work either. I mean, look at the guy." Anthony dribbled the ball a few feet and then threw it to Sam, who tried for a backwards layup shot but missed miserably. "His first job out of college was telemarketing, selling business equipment and making two grand a month. Then he quit that job to work at a car dealership for two months. Who knows what the hell he's up to now?"

Steve and John both ran for the ball, but of course, John grabbed it and easily outran Steve.

"Man, stop bitchin' so much, Anthony!" Steve scoffed, feeling outplayed by John. "You're always complaining about something." Then he looked at John and said, "Are you gonna shoot the fuckin' ball or what?!?"

As sharp in his mind as he was in his athletics, John retorted, "I'm not going to shoot this baby, I'm gonna dunk it right over your head!" Then, moving as quickly as lightning dancing on water, weaving his way through all the other guys, John ran right up to the basket and jumped over Steve. He almost scored a slick dunk shot, but the ball got hung up on the rim and he fell back hard on his ass.

It was so shocking and hilarious that everyone else fell on the ground laughing too.

~ FIVE ~

Anthony PULLED HIS CAR INTO the restaurant parking lot. He hadn't come here because he was in the mood for steamed meat dumplings or Kung Pao Chicken extra spicy. He'd come to meet with his friend Ethan to talk about a killer job opportunity that Ethan said would be perfect for him. Although Anthony didn't really think that Ethan had his act together any more than himself, it wouldn't hurt to talk with him. And he hadn't hung out with Ethan for a few months anyways, so it would be good to catch up and have a few laughs.

Stepping outside of his car, Anthony noticed the few dents it had accumulated over his college tenure, and the paint beginning to crack on the hood. *Jesus Christ*, he thought to himself, *I really ought to get a new ride. I fuckin' hope this job turns out to be cake so I can afford one.* Walking across the parking lot, a few white seagulls screeched as they flew over the roof of the restaurant, probably to the dumpster in the back where they could scavenge a nice meal of Chinese carryout. It was a grey day, "June Gloom" as they call it in Southern California, and Anthony's mood felt about the same. But the air was tranquil and the temperature still bearable, which gave him an underlying feeling of being at ease.

At the front door entrance to the restaurant the words "Golden Dragon" were laminated in bright, thick, gaudy yellow letters on the transparent window pane. *What the hell is it with the Chinese and dragons?* Anthony reflected to himself. *I haven't seen any dragons in Irvine yet. But if I did I'd probably try to catch a ride on one and fly off into the wild blue yonder. It would damn well beat being unemployed!* As he pushed through the door, the sudden appearance of a demure and shapely brown-haired Asian waif startled Anthony out of his ridiculous thoughts.

"Welcome to Golden Dragon!" the pursed ruby red lips of the hostess spoke to Anthony in an Asian accent that had difficulty pronouncing English consonants. "Table for one?"

"Oh, hi," Anthony stammered through a mild embarrassment based on his unconscious fantasy that she had somehow read his thoughts. "No, actually I was meeting a friend for lunch. His name is Ethan Miller. Is he here yet?"

The hostess smiled with a glimmer of attraction at Anthony and, looking down at her ledger, said "Uh, yes he just arrived. Let me walk you over to his table."

"Thank you," Anthony replied with a smile of acknowledgement.

Gracefully plucking another menu from behind her station, the hostess walked stealthily as a cat in her tight black skirt, leading Anthony to Ethan's table. There was a green glass Buddha between the lobby and the main section of the restaurant with both American and Oriental coins at his feet, and intricate golden chimes with red paper figurines hanging from the ceiling. But all Anthony saw was the supple shape of the hostess' ass as it transposed with each mesmerizing step she took. Arriving at the table, the hostess glanced back at Anthony to hand him the menu and noticed he had become enamored with her, and she smiled even more lushly.

As soon as she left, Ethan jumped up from behind his side of the table to give Anthony a hug, exclaiming "Look at this college graduate!"

"How are you bro?" Anthony replied as they hugged.

Sitting down in the booth, Anthony noticed that Ethan wore an expensive Giorgio Armani suit with a colorful tie. He thought this was very unusual for Ethan, and wondered why he was dressed so elaborately.

"Damn homie, you're looking good," Ethan declared through a broad smile. "I see you haven't stopped working out every day."

"You know that will never stop," Anthony retorted confidently. "So, what's up with the suit? Are you the president of some fortune 500 company I don't know about?

"Not yet," Ethan responded. "But, I've got a new job, and the way things are going I won't have to work as long as those guys anyway!"

"Is that right?" Anthony questioned, nodding his head in surprise. "What the fuck are you talking about? Weren't you just selling cars six months ago?"

"Yes, dick-head," Ethan answered laughing. "Thanks for reminding me. But after that I stumbled onto something much better, and that's what I wanted to talk to you about."

At this, Anthony became a little more interested. "Okay, that's cool. But is it legal? 'Cause I don't want to get arrested and end up having some big black guy fuck me in the ass!"

Ethan picked up the menu off the restaurant table and wrinkled his brow. "Yeah, of course it's legal! What's with you and big black guys fucking you in your ass all the time? I don't wanna hear about your secret perverted fantasies dude!"

"Shut the fuck up!" Anthony countered, feeling amused. "I know you better than anyone else, and you cut corners more than I do." Just then a waiter passed by with a plate of flaming duck that sizzled with a striking aroma, briefly sidetracking Anthony from his thoughts. However, he quickly continued, "So tell me, why the fuck are you dressed like some stock broker? Are you trying to sell me a great company to invest money in?"

"No, I'm not man," Ethan replied, feeling frustrated. "I am definitely not a stock broker 'cause I make way more than those bitches, and I work less too."

Anthony could see that Ethan had worked himself up and was getting red in the face. "Okay Buddy," he reassured him. "Calm down and tell me what the fuck you're doing then."

Ethan opened the menu as if he was deciding what to order, then quickly closed it because it only distracted him from his thoughts. "I'm a loan officer," he announced. "Well, actually I'm a mortgage consultant. That's the new title, at least in my office.

"You're doing loans?" Anthony questioned with a disappointed expression of dismay on his face. "How much money could there possibly be in that?"

"Jesus, Anthony!" Ethan protested, slapping his menu down on the table. "There's a fuckin' lot of money in it, that's how much. So shut the fuck up for one second and let me show your dumb ass my check for last month."

Just as Ethan reached into the interior pocket of his suit, the waitress came to take their order. Looking nearly defeated, he said hurriedly, "I'll take the Szechuan Shrimp with wonton soup. What do you want Anthony?"

"Hmmm, you know I haven't really had enough time to look at the menu yet," Anthony replied, obviously trying to fuck with Ethan and make him more impatient.

"Okay, he'll take the same thing as me," Ethan interjected. "And I'm paying," he said to Anthony. "So I hope you don't have a problem with that!"

Anthony laughed, and the waitress looked a little confused. But she took the order and left, leaving Ethan to display his earnings to Anthony. "Check it out, dude," Ethan glowed as he handed Anthony his check.

"Damn!" Anthony exclaimed. "You made twenty grand in one month?" Anthony could barely believe it.

Basking in his own little glory, Ethan appeared quite proud. "Yeah! And I've only been working there for six months!"

Anthony was nearly shocked. "What! Damn homie, that's great. I'm glad you're doing so good now."

"Listen dick-head, I didn't ask you to join me for lunch just to show off my check," Ethan replied with a strangely affectionate tone. "I wanna get you a job at my office. You're way better at sales than I am, and you're gonna blow the fuck up. I just know it!"

As if on cue with Ethan's statement, which had included the words "blow" and "fuck," two beautiful blondes with big fake tits, tight pants and low cut summer shirts walked right by Anthony and Ethan, and were seated at the table next to theirs. Anthony and Ethan's eyebrows raised and their eyes widened, as Anthony checked them out a little longer than a married man probably should.

They both looked at each other and Anthony said "Wow! That's very nice. I'm glad to be back." Returning his attention to Ethan's business proposition, Anthony questioned, "Okay, so what's in this for you? And don't bullshit me, 'cause I've known you since the seventh grade and you never did anything out of the goodness of your own heart."

Without hesitation, Ethan proclaimed, "I get a five percent override on anyone I bring in."

"A five percent override? What's that?"

"Don't worry about that yet, dude," Ethan admonished, as if it wasn't very important. "You haven't even been hired yet. Your interview is on Thursday at nine a.m. sharp. So wear a nice suite, and don't fuck up!"

The waitress returned with the steaming bowls of wonton soup and placed them down in front of Anthony and Ethan. "Thank you," Ethan said to the waitress. Then, picking up his spoon from the table and dipping it into the soup, he looked at Anthony and asked, "So how is that fine ass wife of yours? Is she ready for a real man yet?"

Swallowing his first gulp of soup, Anthony laughed and replied, "Well, we both know you're not talking about *you* being a real man, with that two inch dick of yours."

Overhearing their conversation, the two hot blondes sitting at the table next to theirs laughed, which made Ethan feel embarrassed and go red in the face again. But he was used to this kind of taunting banter with Anthony and quickly brushed it off saying, "I'm glad your back home bro, 'cause we're gonna make a lot of money together. You'll see."

"Yeah, I hope so," Anthony replied, feeling good about Ethan's job opportunity. "I can't keep living off Kelly you know."

"Damn Anthony, I can't believe you just up and got married so young! What a pussy you turned out to be," he exclaimed with a sarcastic grin. "You better wake up man. You're twenty-two years old. You need to party, fuck, and make as much money as you can. Then, by the time you're thirty-five you can settle down." Ethan took a few more gulps of soup as Anthony watched him thinking his way into a speech.

Shaking a little pepper into his bowl, Ethan continued "Remember this, all those little Anthony's you have swimming in your balls don't have an expiration date. Once you hit thirty-five you can still get a hot piece of ass, someone maybe twenty-two or twenty-three years old, and you'll be set for life. You know what I'm saying? I mean, why cash in all your chips now when you can still play your hand?" Looking over at the hot blondes, Ethan gestured to Anthony, "Like with these fine ladies. You were just checking them out. Do you really wanna give that up to some loser who can't even find a wife?"

"Oh, you mean someone like you?" Anthony promptly replied with a sardonic smile. "You know, you really are fucked up in the head! Thanks for the great advice, but I've already sealed the deal with Kelly. And I love her. But I guess you wouldn't know much about love would you?" Anthony wasn't trying to be flat out mean, he was just trying to rub in the fact that Ethan had a hard time finding any kind of lasting relationship. "A guy can't help but look at what's going on in the candy shop. But that doesn't mean he's gotta go in and buy something. That's not me anyway."

"Okay, smart ass!" Ethan retorted. "Once you start making money, we'll see if you have the same plan. Let me tell you something, money changes everyone. Whether you want it to or not."

Having drained their soup bowls clean, the waitress brought the main dish and set both plates down on the table in front of Anthony and Ethan. The shrimp exuded a tantalizing aroma, and they both began to dig in with their mouths watering.

"God damn, I love shrimp," Anthony said after taking his first bite.

"I know you do," Ethan replied. "Once you start working with us, you'll be eating shrimp and lobster every night and drinking champagne for breakfast."

"Yeah, I might need a little champagne to work with you all day!" Anthony laughed.

"You might have to get a little drunk to figure out what to do with all the money you're gonna make working with us!" Ethan countered. "But for now, shut the fuck up and just enjoy your meal. 'Cause the next one is gonna be on you!"

~ SIX ~

ANTHONY LEFT THE RESTAURANT feeling excited about his upcoming job interview with Ethan's company. As a matter of fact, he felt virtually uplifted by the idea that he could start earning some good money very soon. Like any other man, Anthony just wanted to prove himself worthy to the world, and he wanted to provide for his family. After all, a man who can't provide for his family doesn't feel like much of a man. And, although he'd always been a hard worker, he hadn't yet known what it was like to earn a significant paycheck. If what Ethan was telling him was true, this could be a big breakthrough for him, and one worth celebrating.

Although Anthony was basically a good guy who'd never been too selfish or greedy, like just about everyone else who populates this modern capitalistic world, the idea of making lots of money was damn enthralling to him. Hell, from time immemorial mankind has gravitated around the acquisition of power and wealth. For us, money is just the current symbol of that ancient instinct to rise to the top of the pig pile, to procure pleasures and comforts and entertainment of any kind available. Men kill each other every day just to raise their social status a little, to obtain a new material profit, or to support the reign of their own personal empires. We've see it in corporations, in governments, in religious groups and political factions. And although Anthony wasn't interested in hurting anyone, the rush of adrenalin that surged through his veins as he drove his battered, old car on the 5 freeway back to his home was the same as that of any other human being clutching for a little victory in his own personal will to power.

Anthony stopped at the store on the way home to pick up some fresh ingredients for the risotto dish that he and his wife both loved. While he was there he also bought a couple of filet mignon steaks and a fine bottle of pinot noir to compliment the meal. He arrived home in a splendid mood, and walked through the front door whistling a song he had heard on the radio while driving home. He and Kelly had a fairly nice apartment in Irvine. They had decorated it together with art and furniture they'd picked out at the World Market, and with various items that Kelly's parents had brought back from their vacations to Bali, Tahiti, and other far away tropical locations. Under Anthony's guidance, they'd also managed to keep the aesthetic simple and unassuming.

After putting away the groceries and setting the table, Anthony went into the bathroom to wash up. He dabbed on some cologne and got dressed in nice black slacks, a white shirt and a black tie. He wanted to look special for his wife and make her a memorable meal. After this, he walked back into the dining room to retrieve two long-stemmed white candles and placed them in the golden candle holders they had received as a gift at their wedding. He placed them upon the wooden dining table and struck a match to light them. He had always enjoyed making a romantic ambiance for his wife, and he reflected upon the meal he was about to make while appreciating the bright flicker of the flames upon the candles. As he returned to the kitchen to begin preparing the meal, his wife came home. She was dressed professionally, wearing all black and looking as sexy as the day he met her. She carried her business brief case which she put down on the floor by the front door. Surprised to see Anthony in the kitchen looking so debonair, she went immediately to him and embraced him fondly. When she saw the table with the candles burning in the dining room, she looked at him and asked, "What's going on here, baby?"

"What do you mean?" Anthony replied, playing it off like he had nothing in mind. When she looked at him questioningly, he continued, "I'm just making a romantic dinner for the woman I love. Is that okay?"

She felt very happy and gave Anthony another hug, squeezing him tightly against her. Then, pulling back from him, she asked in jest, "And who is that?"

"You baby. Only you," Anthony whispered with a gentle force that simultaneously stirred her heart and her erogenous zones.

With a tender longing in her eyes, Kelly pulled him into her embrace and kissed him deeply. Then she pulled back from him again and said, "Baby, you're so sweet and romantic. Look at you. You even got dressed up all swank and sexy for me." She smiled and glanced briefly towards the kitchen. "Thank you for treating me so special honey. What are you making for dinner?"

"Your favorite! Risotto!" Anthony exclaimed.

"Really? I was gonna make that tonight, too" Kelly said in surprise.

"Well, I beat you to it then," Anthony said with a quick nod, as if to punctuate his statement.

The two of them smiled and gazed into one another's eyes lovingly.

"Wow, baby you really are in a good mood. I'm guessing your lunch date with Ethan went well," Kelly said.

"Yes it did," Anthony said. "But before we talk about it, go change into something a little more comfortable and bring your sexy ass back over here, okay?" Anthony talked to his wife in a seductive voice. Feeling aroused, he pulled her onto him and kissed her ardently, his hand grasping her thigh and moving up under her skirt.

Wanting to postpone his advance, Kelly put her hand on his and pulled it away, saying "Okay, Daddy, let me go change and I'll be right back."

Anthony watched as his wife sauntered into the bedroom and slowly unraveled her attire. First, she peeled off her jacket and kicked off her shoes. Then, she slowly unzipped her skirt and drew it down over her long and sensuous legs. Unbuttoning her blouse to reveal the black lacey bra she wore underneath, upon the long tender slope of her back and the unbearable beauty of her breasts, Anthony could contain his desire no longer. He ran swiftly into the bedroom and seized upon her like a predator in the hot jungle, bending her over the bed and down into an erotic ball of dust.

Minutes, hours, or perhaps an eternity later, they rested upon the crumpled sheets in the afterglow of union. "Honey, that was so good. Can we do that every day when I come home?" Kelly spoke softly as she ran her fingers through Anthony's hair.

"Sure, baby. Anything for you," Anthony replied, feeling nearly sedated.

"So, what happened at your lunch meeting today? I really want to know," she asked him.

"Well, Ethan got me an interview on Thursday at a mortgage company," Anthony replied.

"He did? Wow baby, that's great. What company?"

Anthony stopped to reflect for a moment and realized Ethan hadn't told him the name of the company. "Hmmm, I guess I forgot to ask. And you know how Ethan is, he always leaves out the important stuff," Anthony replied.

"Yeah, I do know how he is baby. But doesn't that worry you just a little bit, not even knowing who he works for?" Kelly inquired.

"No honey, it doesn't. And you shouldn't worry either. Ethan has been my friend for a long time now," Anthony reassured her. "Oh, and guess what? He showed me his check for last month. It was for twenty fuckin' grand!" Anthony exclaimed.

"Holy shit! Really? Is it legal?" Kelly realized she was asking a lot of questions. But she wanted to make sure Anthony got involved in a business venture that was reputable. She knew how eager and sometimes impulsive he was, and her role in the relationship was usually the stabilizing force, while he was the wild one.

Anthony laughed, and said, "Yeah, that's exactly what I asked him, but I guess it's totally on the up and up, from what he said." He kissed her on the forehead and said, "Don't worry baby, I'll find out once I meet the boss, okay? Besides, if this job works out I can get us a better place."

"But I'm fine living here baby!" Kelly protested unexpectedly.

"Well I'm not," Anthony shot right back at her. "And I think your dad might start to like me once I make some real money," he added, bringing up a sore subject of contention between them.

Feeling taken aback, Kelly said, "What do you mean? My dad loves you!"

"No he doesn't," Anthony protested, defending his point of view. "He thinks I just wanna live off of you." Pausing for a moment to collect his thoughts and get hold of his emotions, he continued, "Every time we're over at your folk's place he asks me if I've found a job yet. The way he talks to me and questions me all the time, it's like he's looking down on me." Anthony stopped long enough to notice that Kelly was beginning to feel upset. "Listen," he said, "I don't want to argue about this right now. And anyways, I'm in a really good mood and I don't want to ruin it baby. But I will tell you this, I'll prove it to your dad that I deserve every luscious inch of you."

At this, Kelly's mood brightened and she began to smile again. "Okay baby, okay. You go ahead and prove him wrong," she spoke amorously as she curled around him, kissing and nibbling on his shoulder.

"I sure will. You'll see baby," Anthony replied with confidence.

Stroking his face endearingly, Kelly sat up and said "So, can I please shower now? I had a long day and I skipped lunch too, so I'm starving!"

"Of course you can baby. I'll go get dinner ready right now. But before I do that," he said with a sheepish grin, "I think there's one or two inches I missed."

With this, Anthony ducked under the covers and kissed her all over as Kelly languished in the adoration.

<h1 style="text-align:center">~ SEVEN ~</h1>

THE NEXT FEWS DAYS passed by in their normal rounds without much consequence. Anthony continued to look for a job while Kelly worked. Meals were made, dishes washed, and the garbage got taken out as usual. But in the back of Anthony's mind a spark of new hope had been ignited as he waited in anticipation for the upcoming job interview. He didn't know much about loans, he hadn't even thought much about the salesmen who sell loans, but he knew that when he was on his game he could convince a person to do most anything that was within reason. Maybe his friends were right. Anthony wasn't all that interested in sitting in an office all day doing some company's accounting work. Christ, that really sounded boring. And he had no outstanding aspirations to build a new empire state building like his friend Sam, or an overwhelming humanitarian drive to become a lawyer like Kelly's dad. Truth be told, Anthony just wanted a way to make a good living without compromising himself. And he liked people. He liked talking with people, and he had a keen sense of what was going on in their minds, behind the façade of their shifty eyes and talky talk. In a way, you could say, Anthony thought he sort of knew people from the inside out. Call it a basic instinct, some natural tendency he discovered he had in childhood that he never gave up like most of us do. Anthony could see right through the bullshit to what people really wanted. At least he thought he could.

The morning of the big interview finally came. Kelly arose from sleep as usual and gave Anthony a huge hug, wishing him good luck before she left for work. Anthony showered and dressed in his most impressive suit, slicking his short black hair back very clean. He took a moment to sit down on the bed and collect his thoughts before he left. Although he wasn't exactly religious, Anthony sent out a small prayer to whatever Godlike forces might be looking over him and his life this day, to guide him with the interview, and most importantly, to get him the job. Then he stood up, gathered his brief case and left the house to drive to the interview.

On the way, he stopped for a cup of coffee which he liked almost black with just a little sugar. But he didn't get anything to eat. He was never very hungry in the morning, and he thought more clearly on an empty stomach. Anyways, he suspected his hunger for food might kick in at the interview and increase his impetus to get the job. In fact, Anthony was already very hungry for the job, hungry to make money and establish himself with a respectable position which would make him and his wife happy.

He pulled in to the parking lot of the job interview driving his old beat-up Ford Mustang and looked for a place to park. He was a bit surprised to see so many expensive cars already parked there: Mercedes Benz, BMWs, Porsches, and even a couple of Lamborghini's. It was a bit intimidating and Anthony immediately felt slightly inferior driving his old car; although, he had washed and cleaned it out over the weekend suspecting he might be seen driving in to the interview. He parked on the outer edge of the parking lot to avoid being seen directly. Sitting in the seat, he brushed off his suit and looked in the rear view mirror to make sure his face was clean. Then, taking a deep breath, he got up out of the car holding his brief-case and walked across the parking lot to the job interview entrance.

Anthony entered the front lobby which was rather large and crowded with other young professionals like him who had all come looking for a job. Seeing so many other job seekers, he felt the quickening tension of compe-tition to land the job. Sure he knew Ethan, and Ethan had told him he was a shoe-in for the job, but there were fif-teen, maybe twenty others who had come for the same job as he did. He didn't know how many positions were available, and nothing had been promised to Anthony yet. He'd have to prove himself to earn this job. Looking to-wards the front reception area, Anthony saw an attractive young Mexican receptionist sitting in the enclosed area. Behind her, he saw the company's name, "Fairtex Mort-gage," embossed on the wall in bold golden letters with black encasing.

He approached the receptionist and stood in front of her window. Having seen him when he walked in the door, she quickly looked up at Anthony with an energetic smile, and said, "Hi, can I help you?"

"Yes!" Anthony replied with excitement. "I'm here for the 9:00am interview with David Konn."

"Okay great," she exclaimed. "Let me tell him you're here. Please, have a seat and he will be with you in a moment."

"Thank you very much," Anthony replied with vigor. He then turned around to find a place to sit, and no-ticed that there was only one empty chair in the entire lob-by. He walked over to it and took a seat, putting his brief-case down beside the chair. Looking around him, half in interest and half to size up the competition, Anthony became aware of the overwhelming silence in the room that was filled with so many people. It struck him as somehow humorous—a bunch of flashy people all dressed up fancy sitting in the same room, but almost completely ignoring one another. Everyone appeared to be in his or her own personal world and hardly even made eye contact with anyone else. Not wanting to disrupt the collective trend, Anthony decided just to remain quiet himself and wait for his name to be called. Hopefully it wouldn't be too long.

One by one, other people's names were called and the seats cleared. The room became a little less stuffy, and, as though impelled by the pressure of time, the remaining job interview candidates began to acknowledge one another a little more. Anthony overheard one guy talking about his recent job with a bank in Salem, Massachusetts before the seemingly endless winters sent him scurrying to sunny Southern California to thaw out. He'd heard that story a million times before. Even his own family had come from back East, where the weather was colder in the winter and hotter in the summer. But he knew the nice, warm weather of California came with a price, because everyone wanted to be here. In fact, people migrated in throngs to Southern California, which was why there were so many people there at the interview looking for a job.

Anthony looked up at the lobby clock, which read 9:30am. His own interview appointment time had come and gone, and he was still waiting patiently with the other uncalled candidates. He shifted a bit restlessly in the lobby chair and looked around for a magazine to read while passing the time. He hadn't prepared anything to say to the boss. He was just going in on instinct with this one. *They don't teach you sales in college*, Anthony thought to himself. *It's something you've either got or you don't. And, according to everybody who knows me well, I've got it pretty good.*

"Scott Lawson!" the receptionist's voice called out to the lobby. A young guy with dirty blonde hair verging on red stood up abruptly. Anthony could see the nervous awkwardness in the guy's face and in the way he walked to the door and fumbled with the handle before going in. *He won't last long,* Anthony thought.

With each name called, Anthony had an initial surge of hope that it would be his own, followed by an increasingly painful pang of disappointment when it was not. Indeed, it was nearly 10:00am and his name had not yet been called. He looked around at the other few remaining candidates who all appeared to be growing both worried and weary with the wait. *Ah, what the hell,* he thought to himself. *They can't ignore me for long, not with Ethan working here and referring me in.* Feeling confident that his name would soon be called, Anthony resolved to just bide his time and watch all the people stream by as if he were watching a movie in which he knew there would be a happy ending.

And so he did. And the lobby emptied more until only he and one other candidate remained. *Yup, I bet they're saving the best for last!* Anthony encouraged himself. Then, having waited for almost 2 hours, he looked up to see the lobby clock which nearly read 10:30am, and heard the receptionist's voice called out "Anthony Cousto!"

"Yes!" Anthony promptly replied, as he stood up from his seat and grabbed his briefcase.

"Mr. Konn will see you now. Will you please follow me?"

"I sure will," Anthony replied as he walked through the lobby and opened the door to the other side, to what he'd come for and been waiting for so long. He followed the receptionist across the expansive sales room floor which contained a great many office cubicles all buzzing with the voices of sales people working the phones and chatting to each other about loans. Amidst the nearly one hundred workers who filled the sales room floor, Anthony saw his friend Ethan who waved to him with a look of encouragement and give him the thumbs up. Anthony smiled and continued to follow the receptionist to the other side of the room, where a row of offices lined the far wall. They walked to the door that read: Office Manager, DAVID KONN, and she knocked. Upon hearing a response, she opened the door and told Mr. Konn that Anthony Cousto was there for his interview. Then she motioned for Anthony to enter, whereupon Mr. Konn stood up from behind his desk and said, "Welcome Anthony! Come in and have a seat."

"Thank you, sir," Anthony replied, as Mr. Konn came over briefly and gave him a warm handshake. He thanked the receptionist for having brought Anthony to his office, and she left closing the door behind her.

Mr. Konn was tall and a little overweight, but nonetheless had an imposing physical presence. With light blonde hair that was beginning to thin out on the top of his head, he wore stylish reading glasses with dark brown rims. He was clean shaven, appeared to be somewhere in his mid-thirties, and dressed in an elaborate 3-piece striped suit with a platinum Rolex watch. Anthony noticed that Mr. Konn moved with the briskness of a salesman eager to do business. Occupying his office was a lengthy and very busy desk with an impressive computer monitor fixed upon it. To Anthony, he looked like an important man.

Sitting back down on his chair and gathering together Anthony's job application and other relevant interview papers he had at hand, Mr. Konn looked up and said, "So Anthony, Ethan told me some great things about you."

"Oh he did? We've been friends for a long time. He's a great guy!"

"And a damn good salesman too, I might add!"

Knowing his friend all too well, Anthony couldn't help smiling, and proclaimed, "Yes he is, Mr. Konn."

"Do you want to know one of the things Ethan told me about you?" Mr. Konn asked.

"Sure," Anthony replied, not knowing what to expect.

"He said that you're ten times better at sales then he is. Is that true?"

"Well, I don't know about ten times better, but to be honest with you, I think we're pretty close."

"Great answer," Mr. Konn exclaimed. "I'm glad you're not cocky like Ethan. He's a good guy, but sometimes he can be so full of himself that I wonder if he came with an emergency deflate button just to make sure he won't pop!"

Anthony and David both laughed, and Anthony reciprocated Mr. Konn's sentiment, "Yes, I know what you mean."

After their laughter subsided, Mr. Konn became slightly serious and said, "Listen Anthony, I'd like to do this interview a little bit differently with you than with the other people." He looked away briefly, at something through his office window, then returned his gaze to Anthony and asserted, "You seem like the kind of guy that's pretty straight up! Am I right about that?"

"Yes, sir. I think I am," Anthony agreed.

"And you don't like to bullshit, do you?"

"No, sir. I don't."

"Okay, great!" Mr. Konn appeared to be impelled by some unseen source of energy. "So tell me, why do you want to work here?"

Anthony was surprised by this question, and didn't really knew how to answer it. *Jesus*, he thought to himself, *I just want to work here to make some fuckin' money.* But he also wanted to please the boss, so out loud he said to Mr. Konn, "Um, I'd like to help people get home mortgages and assist them with their refinancing needs."

His comment was immediately met with a frown of disappointment from Mr. Konn, followed by a slight chuckle. "Anthony, I thought we agreed to not bullshit?" Mr. Konn reminded him. "Come on, that's not why you're sitting in that chair. So, I will ask you one more time; why do you want to work here?"

Anthony looked down briefly at his nice dress pants and at the red carpet that had been well-worn with the flux of business. For just a second he felt put upon and confused, like he had somehow been duped by this whole affair. Then, just as quickly, it occurred to him that he should take the risk of speaking the truth. "Honestly, Mr. Konn, I'm here because I wanna make money!" he exclaimed.

Mr. Konn's demeanor shifted completely as he was both relieved and overjoyed that Anthony had been assertive around why he wanted to work for him. If a salesman can't assert himself he isn't any good, and Mr. Konn had put everyone he hired to the same test to make sure he knew they had enough balls to get the job done. Getting down to business, he began to talk to Anthony with a sense of immediacy, launching upon a great exposé of the company which bordered on a rant.

"Okay great," he exclaimed. "This is the place to do it. There is only one reason why people work here. And that's money. Nothing else. No one give's a fuck about a loan or making someone else happy, unless it makes you money—that's just bullshit you tell everyone else about your job! Don't work here if you want to do good in this world. This is not the place for that Red Cross shit. There's no salary here, no paid leave, and no medical or dental benefits. We don't do things like corporate America. You make your own dreams here. Some people here make nothing, and if you do that two months in a row you're fuckin' out! We have no time here for turds. Do you understand what I'm saying Anthony?"

"Yes, sir" Anthony exclaimed, feeling excited and inspired by the brashness of Mr. Konn's speech.

"Good. Now to some news that might further motivate you. The average loan officer here makes at least twenty thousand dollars a month. That's out of one hundred and five loan officers. Some make nothing, and the highest check I've seen in one month is two hundred and forty-five thousand. Stand up and look out the window behind you."

Anthony stood up to look out the office window into the shuffling commotion of the sales floor.

"You see that guy over there with the pink shirt walking around like he has a ten-inch cock?"

Anthony broke-out out with a sudden jolt of laughter, saying "Yes, I see him."

"He was the highest paid loan officer last year! Can you guess what he made?"

"Hmmm," Anthony racked his brain to come up with a good figure. "I'd say somewhere around seven hundred thousand dollars."

"Nope!" Mr. Konn countered. "Over one million. Do you believe that? You can sit down now Anthony."

"Now, do you wanna guess how old he is?" Mr. Konn continued.

"Maybe thirty-five," Anthony replied.

"He's just twenty-seven years old," Mr. Konn retorted. "You see Anthony, you can make all of your dreams come true here. All of them. It just depends on how hard you are willing to work." Leaning back in his black leather chair, Mr. Konn continued, "The doors open every day at six a.m. and don't close until nine p.m. You can come and go as you please. But every Tuesday at nine a.m. sharp we have a meeting that you have to attend." He paused to give Anthony a few moments to take it all in. "So, what do you think? Is this the job opportunity you're looking for Anthony?"

Without skipping a beat, Anthony replied, "Yes, sir. It definitely is."

"Okay, great. That's what I like to hear!" Mr. Konn was happy that all his hot breath had paid off. Looking at Anthony he suspected he had just recruited a new heavy hitter. "If you're half as good as Ethan says, you will do amazingly well. Your first day is Monday at eight a.m. for orientation. I'm going to put you on the same team as Ethan so he can help you out at first. Any questions?" he asked.

"No sir. Thank you very much," Anthony replied. "And I promise I won't let you down."

"Good! 'Cause if you do, I will personally fire you myself." Mr. Konn laughed as he said this, but they both knew he was being dead serious.

"I understand, Mr. Konn," Anthony acknowledged.

After saying this, Mr. Konn stood up from behind his desk and walked around to shake Anthony's hand. "Great! It was nice to finally meet you Anthony. Welcome to the team. I have a feeling you're going to fit in perfectly."

"Thanks again, Mr. Konn. I really appreciate it," Anthony said.

After shaking hands, Mr. Konn opened the door for Anthony and he walked out onto the busy sales room floor. As he walked across the room towards the other side of the building, his friend Ethan spotted him and came over quickly to ask him how the interview went.

"I got it!" Anthony beamed. "I start on Monday at eight a.m."

"That's awesome man!" Ethan declared. "So, whose team are you gonna be on?"

"Your team dude," Anthony smiled.

"Fuck yeah, bro! We have the sickest team ever," Ethan said with great excitement. "We don't do a lot of loans, but we charge the most and that's all that counts anyway. I would introduce you to a couple of the guys, but they don't come in this early most of the time."

"Really? What do you mean, it's almost eleven thirty!"

"You have a lot to learn my friend!" Ethan retorted. "Oh, and tell that fine ass girl of yours I said 'Hi.'"

"Yeah, I sure will asshole!" Anthony said, rejoining the normal one-upmanship banter he and Ethan had traded in good fun for years.

"Whatever! I have to get back to a client I have on hold. Do you want to go out this weekend?" Ethan asked him. Then, answering his own question he added, "Oh yeah, I forgot you're married. I guess I'll see you on Monday then homie!"

"Yeah, I'll see you on Monday. Try not to be too hung over or you'll forget to show me what to do!" Anthony cajoled.

He and Ethan shook hands, and Ethan walked back to his desk becoming obviously enticed by the ass of a female worker who was slightly bent over using the Xerox machine. He looked back at Anthony, smiling like a little kid at the playground, and Anthony continued to walk towards the exit door laughing.

<h1 style="text-align:center">~ EIGHT ~</h1>

AFTER GETTING THE JOB, Anthony was elated. He was thinking about all the things that would change in his life once he had some real money. To celebrate, that night he took Kelly out to a classy bar for cocktails. The place was nicely situated, with a view of the affluent downtown district, the businesses and homes of the elite, which shone and sparkled in the night like electric jewels suspended in the sky. As they sat sipping their drinks, she loved cosmopolitans and Anthony enjoyed a strong margarita, he shared his dream of moving up in the world, of buying a nice home like those in their view, of having the good things in life like vacations and sports cars and a swimming pool in the back yard.

"You see Kelly," Anthony said to her, "I want to make you happy by giving you the best things in life." He looked down at his drink for a moment, as if remembering something, and continued. "When we first met I was just a scrappy college kid, but I want you to know what I'm really made of. This job is my big chance to show you. I'm going to take care of you the way you really deserve. I'm going to be the man who makes your dreams come true, Kelly. Just wait and you'll see."

She smiled lovingly at him and took another sip of her drink. She knew how much Anthony loved her, how intensely devoted he was to her and to making her happy.

"I know sweetheart," she said. "But remember, you already are the man of my dreams. And you've already made me more happy than I could have imagined."

"Well good!" Anthony exclaimed boldly. "It's only going to get better baby."

They drank a few more drinks that night and walked around the city streets reminiscing about their early college days. They were both very happy and excited about Anthony's upcoming job. Kelly didn't care as much about the money as Anthony did, but she felt both charmed and deeply reassured by the veracity of his intent to earn a good living. Later that night they had sex. She could feel something in his movements that had relaxed, that had given in to her, surrendered and opened up. The tension Anthony had been feeling about finding a job had partially dissolved; he was relieved while at the same time strengthened by the job offer. He had needed a channel into which he could express his energies, and now he felt he had found it.

Anthony arrived back at the Fairtex Mortgage office early Monday morning, eager to start the new job. He smiled at the receptionist as he walked through the front lobby, and said "Good morning!" Although he was a bit nervous about beginning the new job, he felt a sense of pride and accomplishment at having passed the interview as he greeted her. This time, he also considered himself as part of the company, so his demeanor was more confident and assertive.

"Good morning, Mr. Cousto," the receptionist responded. Anthony was surprised that she remembered his name.

Holding his brief case in one hand and his coffee in the other, he said to her with a smile, "I was hired last Thursday and told to return for the orientation meeting this morning."

"Yes, sir. Mr. Konn has informed me to direct you to the meeting room. Please come around through the door and I'll show you there," she said to him politely.

Anthony opened the lobby door into the sales room floor area and followed the receptionist to the meeting room. She opened the door to the meeting room, smiled, and wished him a good day. After thanking her, Anthony proceeded into the meeting room which was beginning to fill up with some of the people he had seen the previous week in the lobby. This time, having progressed from a status of job candidates in competition to that of fledgling team members, Anthony observed that the people appeared to be more interested in one another and were all making small talk. He took a seat at the large meeting table and joined in.

One by one, new hires filled the room until the table was fully surrounded by bright, shining faces all ready to learn about their new jobs. Anthony noticed there were only four women in the group; however, the most beautiful one sat down right next to him. The table buzzed with chatter and the anticipation of the group became palpable until suddenly a man no one recognized opened the door abruptly and with a sense of purpose. Standing before them, he exclaimed with a very serious and authoritative tone, "Good morning everyone! I'm Brian Skidmore."

The entire room silenced immediately, as the group of new hires restrained themselves from expressing amusement at the graphic humor of Brian's last name.

Knowing full well the common response everyone had to his name, Skidmore continued, "I might have a funny last name to you, but I'm the most important person you have to help you get on the right track here. If you fuck up with me and don't pay attention, then you're pretty much fucked."

The atmosphere of the room quickly changed from light and airy to very tense and focused, as no one had expected the orientation to begin like this. Everyone's attention centered on Skidmore, and a feeling of foreboding and awe filled the new hires.

"Eighty percent of you won't be here after the next sixty days, not because you don't want to, but because you've been fired," Skidmore said blatantly, alarming the group. "We only keep the best here. Fairtex Mortgage is one of the largest mortgage brokers in California. Not in size, but in production. Collectively, we do over three hundred loans a month. Some of our loan officers do twenty-five loans a month and some do zero. If you do zero, you better look for a new job. We have a very high turnover rate, which means we are always hiring someone to take your spot. So please don't think we need you." Skidmore had a deadpan expression on his face which some of the new hires thought was also ruthless as he talked to the group.

Shit, Anthony thought to himself. *This guy is a fuckin' monster*. But, in truth, he was thoroughly impressed with Brian's forceful honesty and directness. *It's kinda like the military*, he thought. *Boot camp for salesmen!*

"However, if you do well, this position can be very rewarding," Skidmore continued. "We have contests every month, trips to Vegas, Maui, Cabo, golf tournaments, box seats at Laker games, as well as prime tickets to baseball and football games. We also have a monthly dinner for the top ten producing loan officers. To top it off, if you do really fuckin' well, Fairtex Mortgage will buy you a car!" A low-volume response arose from the group collectively like a sonic fog rising up from the floor and quickly dissipated into the hum of the room. "That's right people, a goddamn car. And I'm not talking about some used piece of shit or a KIA. I'm talking about a BMW, Mercedes, or Porsche. As long as the payment is over a thousand dollars a month! So you're all probably thinking, 'What do I have to do to get that?' Right?"

For better or worse, the new hires were all shocked by Skidmore's unexpected bombast. Some wondered if they should run like hell and some were chomping at the bit to get to work. A few had heard this kind of spiel before and weren't exactly impressed with it, but moreover suspicious because they'd been burned before by a lot of hype and fast talk. Anthony maintained his composure, interested in the proposition of making buku bucks and winning a new car, but not wanting to appear overly eager or anxious. He had seen the kind of guy who was overly-eager to please, and he didn't want to look like anybody's bitch. So he remained alert but calm, and waited for Skidmore to continue.

"You have to rev sixty-five grand for three months straight," Brian answered his own question. Then he continued with a smug inflection, "Let's see how smart you people are; who knows what rev is?"

The attractive brunette sitting next to Anthony quickly spoke out, "Revenue!"

"Correct! That's how we make money people. Revenue!" Skidmore's voice boomed back into the room.

Upon hearing this response, the woman sitting next to Anthony glanced briefly at him with a joyful look of gratification. Anthony was happy for the pleasant distraction and smiled back at her with an approving nod.

"Revenue is the only fuckin' thing we give a shit about. Do you guys want to know what we don't like here?" Skidmore made an ugly facial gesticulation as he hollered out, "LOSERS! Fuck losers. Losers can go work at some bullshit job making sixty grand a year with vacation time, a 401k and health-care. Fuck that! If you want the typical benefits, then you might as well get the fuck out of this office right now and save me the time."

Hearing this, the more sensitive-hearted new hires squirmed in their seats and a few thought about bolting right away. But none did, because they were too afraid of being ridiculed on the way out. Anthony didn't much care about the macho bravado crap. In truth, he kind of liked a good confrontation because it made him more aware of his own strength and inertia.

"Losers call in sick," Skidmore ranted on. "Losers say, 'I'm sorry, I can't do it because the other company's rates are so much better than ours.' Losers work three hours a day and take two hour lunch breaks. Fuck those turds! As a matter of fact, most of you in here *are* turds. Well, you haven't proven as much yet, but your true colors will come out in the next sixty days. So, if you don't want me to call you a turd, then prove me wrong in the coming weeks." Brian finally let up and relaxed a little. "Okay guys, that was the negative stuff. Do you want me to tell you about the positive things we look for?"

The room full of new hires gave a collective response of affirmation.

"People who just do it and shut the fuck up!" Brian roared, shocking them even more. Then he added, "Those people stay after hours to work and they don't leave until they have at least three applications every day. They work on weekends and, most importantly, they pay attention to what the fuck we say, 'cause if you can't even do that what's the point of working here? You might as well go work at Wal-Mart and just greet people as they walk in the door. That's a fuckin' easy job, right?"

No one in the room said anything this time. They didn't know if Skidmore was taunting them or encouraging them.

"Now! Anyone have any questions?" Skidmore continued.

The new hires remained quiet, although there was an aura of discomfort in the room, mixed with a strange kind of excitement. It was like the feeling one got when a fight broke out and no one knew exactly what was going to happen.

"Okay good," Skidmore broke the silence. "Now here's the lowdown. You guys get a forty-five percent split of the leads we provide you. Seventy percent if you find your own clients. Everyone in here has got to have their real estate license within five months. If you don't have it, you're done here. I don't care how much money you make us! Clear? Good!"

The barrage of facts kept coming like a hail storm against the vulnerable minds of the new hires which had already been thoroughly marinated in Skidmore's expletives. "All of you are going to be assigned a Sales Manager. Their sole purpose is to help you succeed. One word of advice, listen to what they say. All sales managers were once top producing loan officers, and they have all made more money than you can dream of. Don't listen to some fat fuck who's been here seven weeks and hasn't even taken an application, 'cause he won't be here the next week. Choose wisely about who you take your advice from."

A few of the new hires laughed nervously and looked at each other, wondering when this guy was going to run out of steam. Or if he ever would. Anthony glanced around the table and sized up the other employees. He thought if anyone in the room could live up to Skidmore's expectations, he could. In fact, the long-winded diatribe on sales had made him feel taut inside, like a sling shot pulled back and ready to be released. The four long years of college, culminating in a string of bad job interviews had led him to this one golden opportunity. He had the smarts, the people skills, and the motivation to let loose with this. And now he knew he would.

"In the next two weeks," Skidmore continued, "you're going to learn about everything. It will probably be the most intensive training period you've ever lived through, that's if you make it. Now, what I'd like each one of you to do is go and introduce yourself to your Sales Managers. After that, you can hang out if you want or go home, it's up to you. Our first real day won't start until tomorrow. So please, just think about what I said today. If you don't show up tomorrow, no hard feelings, this just wasn't for you. But if you come to work tomorrow, please give me everything you have, and I promise you won't fail."

At that, Skidmore stood up straight and walked out of the room, leaving all the new hires soaked in a tangible bath of astounded bewilderment.

~ NINE ~

IN THE DIN AND THE MURMUR of the orientation meeting room, Anthony looked over to the woman sitting beside him and introduced himself.

"Wow! That guy is something, huh?" he said.

"Yeah, he sure is" she replied. Then laughing in relief that the meeting was over, she added, "I bet someone didn't hug him enough as a kid!" Anthony laughed too, as she introduced herself, saying, "Hi, I'm Jessica Taylor."

"Nice to meet you," Anthony replied. "I'm Anthony Cousto. So your sales manager is Frankie Lister, too?

"Yup," Jessica said. "I hope he's nicer than Skidmore."

"Me too," Anthony exclaimed.

Jessica Taylor was a light-skinned Mexican and a native of Irvine with the voice of a valley girl. She was great to look at, well-proportioned with nice curves in all the right places. And she had a pleasant personality and was easy to talk to. Jessica had grown up in a semi-affluent family with a father who worked in the upper management division of RCA. He had started when all they sold was televisions, but remained over the years to see the company boom into the multimedia electronics maker they are today. At any rate, the job had afforded him a nice paycheck, and the luxury of having lived a comfortable life could be read on Jessica's face. She was at ease with herself and was not easily disturbed. At least, she had survived Brian Skidmore's interrogation welcome meeting with her sense of humor intact. In fact, she did not appear to have been perturbed whatsoever by the unusually provocative orientation meeting. Quite to the contrary, her face glowed and her cheeks pinkened as she exchanged trivialities with Anthony regarding the prospect of the job.

As they briefly became acquainted, Anthony thought Jessica was both genuine and pretty. He noticed the depth of her brown eyes which held a certain luster, and the sophisticated manner of her dress which was both feminine and professional without being overly-revealing like some women who appear to wear nothing but lingerie to work. Although he definitely enjoyed the cleavage, it could be a bit distracting on the job, and he appreciated a measure of modesty.

After talking a few minutes, Anthony and Jessica realized they better get a move on it to meet with their sales manager. On the way out of the meeting room, they ran into the third new hire that was on their sales team. A bit short and overweight, Hector had inquisitive brown eyes and an honest face. As the name implies, he was of Latino descent. Like Anthony, he had not been raised in a wealthy home, but had moved to Irvine as a child with his parents who sought a better life in America. He too, was at the vanguard of his family and the first to receive a college degree or to work a job which required wearing nice clothes. Unlike Anthony, Hector and his family had come from Mexico, so Hector was a first generation Mexican-American. So far, he had done a good job of integrating American culture into his personal identity while remaining faithful to his own original culture and family, many of whom were still in Mexico or only spoke Spanish. It was at times a tenacious balancing act, and a confusing one which involved wearing multiple masks and playing different roles. But Hector had an even temperament and tended to be the peacemaker in most situations. After the tirade inflicted upon him by Skidmore, Hector wasn't sure if he was cut out for sales, but he was determined to give it his best shot. After all, the great thing about America, he had been told, was that everyone had the same opportunity to achieve success.

Anthony, Jessica, and Hector walked across the sales room floor looking for the office of their new sales manager. Reaching the other side, they looked at the names on the doors until they found the name Frankie Lister. Anthony took the lead and knocked on the door, and they all three looked at each other with a wide-eyed expression of uncertainty, wondering if this guy would be as extreme and belligerent as the last.

"Come in!" a coarse voice resounded loudly through the closed door.

They opened the door and proceeded into the office to see a nerdy looking guy with a buzz haircut and thick glasses sitting behind a very cluttered desk. His hair was so short it could only be described as dark, and his eyes were a blisteringly bright blue. He had a few horizontal lines in his face, on his forehead and around his eyes. Lines that indicated experience and longevity, and made him look serious. Like the other managers, he was dressed in an expensive suit and emanated an aloof and distinguished aura. Only he was super sharp, not a wrinkle in his suit or one iota of lint or any other such defilement upon his attire. He also looked as if he was very physically fit beneath the suit and talked in a highly regimented manner, as if he may have at some point been in the Marines.

As they all filed into the room and stood waiting for his recognition, he talked angrily on the phone.

"Just fund the fuckin' loan, okay! I don't care how you do it," his voice blasted into the receiver. "But by noon, it better be done!"

Then he slammed the phone down into its holder and looked up at the three new recruits. "So," he said with a raspy wornness in his voice that inferred he had been through this process many times before, "you guys are my new fishes, eh? Well, let's just hope you're better than my last three, 'cause they didn't even last thirty days."

"Yes sir, we just came from the orientation meeting," Anthony said, speaking up for the group. "Mr. Skidmore informed us that we should see you."

"Hmmm. Well, you made it through Skidmore, so I guess you're all serious about the job." Before any of the them had time to answer, Lister continued, "So check it out guys, I'm really busy today and I can't talk long. Here's what I want you three to do."

As if he suddenly became sidetracked from his original idea, Lister looked at Hector and asked "What's your name?"

"Hector Gomez, sir."

Feeling annoyed and impatient with obsequious formalities, Lister shot back, "Okay, first thing I want you to do is never call me sir. Understood?"

The three new hires nodded their heads up and down in agreement.

"Call me Frankie, okay?" At this he nearly smiled, but scared himself with the alluring profundity of his own mirth and resumed being serious. "Hector, you see that black guy out there?" he continued, pointing out the open office door to one of the few African American workers on the sales floor. "His name is Lamar."

"Yes," Hector replied.

Lamar was the king of cool. He never let anything bother him, unless it was a matter of losing a shitload of money. He moved languidly around the office, slowly with a sense of deliberation and purpose. He never seemed to be in a rush or to force anything. In the office atmosphere of frenetic ramblings and cacophony, Lamar provided a sense of balance, a reference point for sanity. Other workers naturally gravitated towards him when they were stressed out or needing to calm down. It was the same at the bar with the ladies. Lamar exuded a reassuring presence that was like gravity to a woman's heart. He never had to try very hard, or really try at all, because the women would flow to him like syrup running down the side of a stack of hotcakes.

"Right now everyone is doing what we call Power Hours. It's basically non-stop telemarketing for three hours. Go sit next to him and just listen to his conversation."

"Okay, Mr. Lister," Hector said, and he walked over to sit down and listen to his new mentor.

Lister then looked at Jessica and said, "And what's your name, sweetheart?"

"I'm Jessica, suh.." Jessica began to say sir, but caught herself and said, "Mr. Lister."

"Okay, nice to meet you Jessica. See that terrorist looking guy out there?" Lister smiled sourly as if he had made a bad joke. "His name is Al. I want you to go sit next to him and pay close attention to his phone conversations, 'cause he's real good. But whatever you do Jessica, don't let him sweet talk you."

"Okay. Thanks Mr. Lister," Jessica said, and walked over to sit down by Al.

Frankie then looked at Anthony and said "You have your buddy Ethan to learn from, okay. I'm sure you won't mind hangin' out with him for a couple of hours to hear how he works."

"No, Mr. Lister, I sure won't," Anthony replied.

"For Christ sake call me Frankie!" Lister shot back at him. "Now listen Anthony, before you guys leave today," Lister motioned to Anthony as well as Jessica and Hector when he said this. "I want you to write down your cell phone numbers and leave them on my desk. I can see that you're the leader of this little troupe, so I want you to fill them in on something, okay?"

Anthony nodded as Lister continued talking.

"Over the next thirty days I'm going to call and harass you guys every day to make sure you're learning the job and selling loans. I don't care if you're brushing your teeth or taking a shit or out late at night gettin' laid, you had better pick up the fuckin' phone. Understand?" Lister looked at Anthony with hard steel and a undeterminable amount of craziness in his eyes.

Anthony smiled, and swiftly replied with optimism, "Yes!"

"Okay, good!" Lister barked. "Now go!"

~ TEN ~

ANTHONY WALKED STRAIGHT from Lister's office over to his friend Ethan's cubicle. The whole sales room floor was teaming with the enthusiastic voices of sales people talking to customers, explaining loans and negotiating deals. The sense of adventure and commerce was so thick in the air that Anthony felt like he was swimming in it. Arriving at the other side of the sales room floor, Ethan's cubicle was a virtual mass of sticky notes and papers all splayed at odd angles, as Ethan sat slightly leaned back in his chair, his legs spread out over the carpet, immersed in a phone conversation with a customer. When Anthony approached, he placed his hand on Ethan's shoulder to let him know he was there. Ethan knew the drill well, and he motioned for Anthony to take a seat and put on a set of headphones so that he could listen in on Ethan's conversation with the customer.

"Sorry to put you on hold Ms. Lewis," Anthony listened to Ethan's phone conversation through the headphones. "I just spoke with the lock desk and I was able to beat the rate you were offered by the bank!"

"Oh really, God that's great news," Ms. Lewis replied. "What rate were you able to get?"

"Well, the bank offered you 6.25% on a 30 year fixed rate," said Ethan. "But we can get you 5.62% on the same program! How does that sound?" This was just the beginning of the deception process with which Ethan had become quite adept.

"That would be really great Ethan. How much are you charging for the fees?" Ms. Lewis asked.

"That's the best part, Ms. Lewis. The bank was charging you $1,500 which is half a point, right?"

"Yes," she replied.

"Well, with us you're getting a lower rate and we're only charging 1 point, which is $3,000. So, basically, with the bank your fees were a little less, but you were paying for it in the higher payment or rate, which means that over time the loan from the bank would cost you a lot more than the $1,500 they were charging you."

To amuse Anthony, Ethan acted like he was punching numbers on his hand.

"I just punched in the numbers Ms. Lewis, and it shows that I'm saving you over $45,000 in the next 30 years compared to the bank's loan."

With this final explanation Ethan had delivered the death blow to the customer. An offer she could not refuse. Although it was all bullshit, presenting her repayment situation as well as he did had convinced her. After saying this, Ethan expressed his theatrical verve by standing up and moving his hips back and forth as if he was fucking someone doggy style, obviously intended to denote how well he was screwing the customer.

"Really? That's amazing Ethan. Are you sure you can get me this loan? Even when I'm not currently working?" Ms. Lewis inquired.

Ethan high-fived Anthony with a huge smile of mischievous victory. Anthony smiled too, and felt a surge of appreciation and acknowledgement for how well Ethan had landed the loan.

"Oh definitely, Ms. Lewis. I wouldn't lie to you ma'am," Ethan falsely reassured her.

"Okay, great. Well then let's do it!" Ms. Lewis replied eagerly. "I'll call the bank and cancel with them right now."

"Wonderful, Ms. Lewis. I'll transfer you to my secretary and she'll let you know what documents we need. Take care Ms. Lewis. Talk to you soon."

Ethan punched in the transfer button and flung the headphones off his head onto the desk. Then he stood up excitedly, held up an open hand in front of him and moved it rapidly down towards his crotch while yelling out, "Boooooom!"

Everyone on the sales room floor turned briefly towards the sound of Ethan's voice and smiled. They all knew this was the Lister team's ritual celebration of landing a loan. However, it was all new to Anthony, who simply looked on in amazement.

Upon hearing Ethan, Lister came rushing out of his office and exclaimed "Fuck yeah, bro! That's what I'm talking about Ethan. You see that shit Anthony? That's how you do it. Alright! Good fuckin' job Ethan. Keep up the good work!"

Lister looked around at the other sales people who had taken note of his loud and demonstrative fanfare with Ethan. "Everyone else keep hittin' the fuckin' phones 'cause it's Power Hours! You better get three apps before you even think about going home!" Then he walked back into his office and slammed the door.

Ethan turned to look at Anthony who was smiling and in shock, mouth agape and speechless.

He sat down next to him laughing and said almost in a whisper, "Okay, let me tell you what I'm doing. On our team, every time you sell a loan or fund one, you have to do that whole boom routine. If you don't and Lister catches you, you're fucked!"

"What?" Anthony replied, obviously confused.

"Shit, let me try to explain it to you," Ethan continued. "We have a tradition on our team. I know it looks really stupid, but Lister takes it very seriously. He thinks that's why our team has been #1 every month for the last year. It's a major deal to him."

"Okay," Anthony said, listening with curiosity.

"Lemme tell you a story so you can understand this shit," said Ethan. "About thirteen or fourteen months ago this new guy comes in to work with us. He funds his first loan, but forgets to do the god damn 'boom routine. That month our team did the worst in the whole fuckin' office. So Lister takes the guy out for a couple drinks and gets the poor fuck wasted off his ass. The fuckin' kid just moved here from the east coast, so Lister wanted to break him in by taking him to a biker bar."

Anthony chuckled as Ethan told him the story, wondering what would happen next.

"Then, Lister pays this big fuckin' biker dude a thousand bucks to pick a fight with the guy outside the bar. Then he goes to the bathroom, so later he can tell the guy he didn't even see what happened. So the biker drags the guy out to the back alley and fucks him up so bad he's knocked out cold on the street. But that's not the end of it. Lister, with his sick and twisted imagination, wanted to really fuck the guy up in the head. So after the biker dude leaves him in the alley, Lister goes out and pulls the guy's pants down just below his ass. He pulls a condom out of his wallet, unwraps it and just tucks it in the guy's butt cheeks. So when the guy wakes up, Lister is like 'Hey man, what the hell happened? And why do you have a condom hanging out your ass dude?' Completely freaked the guy the fuck out. He never came back to work."

"God damn," Anthony replied in disbelief. "What the fuck! What happened to the poor guy?"

"I don't know! Word is he was so embarrassed that he packed his shit, and moved back to the east coast. Fuckin' crazy, huh?"

"Jesus Christ, you can say that!" Anthony exclaimed apprehensively.

"No shit! Lister is a straight up crazy ass marine! The guy smokes two packs a day, drives a piece of shit truck, and lives by himself. No wife, no family, and no furniture, just a couch and TV. That's it. And he drinks from the moment he gets home. The weird part is, the guy makes over forty grand a month, and nobody knows what he does with all his money."

"Damn, that's a lot of moolah" Anthony replied. "I fuckin' know what I would do with it if I made that much," he said laughing. Then, referring to Ethan's phone conversation, he asked, "So, did you really lock Ms. Lewis at 5.625%?"

"Fuck no!" Ethan exclaimed, leaning forward and shuffling through the loan document papers on his desk. He found what he was looking for, then leaned back in his chair again to explain it all to Anthony. "That rate's not even available to her. She has no job, which means we need to make one up for her. On top of it all, she's been late for the last two months. Some fuckin' idiot at another broker shop is offering her a 6.25%, knowing he can't get that, so we'll play the same game and offer her a lower rate than him. Once the real documents get printed, I'll sell her on a 7.0% adjustable and charge her ass max fees, which is gonna be like fifteen grand. By that time, she'll have no choice but to sign. That's the game we play." Ethan smiled with a feeling of victory. Then he stood up and said, "C'mon, let me show you around the office and introduce you to a few of the players on our team."

Anthony followed Ethan over to the small lunch room area across the room from the cubicles. Ethan opened the refrigerator and pulled out a couple of sparkling waters, then handed one to Anthony. Looking back across the room to the cubicles, Ethan nodded his head in the direction of Hector and said, "You see that black guy who is showing one of the other new hires on our team how this is done?"

"Yeah," Anthony nodded.

"His name is Lamar, and his specialty is single female homeowners. That's pretty much all he does for some reason. When he was in his twenties, he did five years for transportation. He can't get his Real Estate license, so the big man pays him under the table 'cause the guy makes around twenty to fifty grand a month."

Hearing this, Anthony tried not to shit his pants. Just a couple weeks ago he had been working slop in a Mexican restaurant, struggling to earn his college degree. And now he was in a room full of loaded sales guys who were breaking the bank. The sudden change was staggering to him.

"You see that guy next to Lamar blowing his nose?" Ethan continued. "His name is Kevin, but we call him 'Snowman.' And he's not blowing his nose 'cause he has a cold, I can tell you that," Ethan smirked. "Fuckin' guy goes to the bathroom every fifteen minutes to do blow. He gambles on every fuckin' thing he can, from ping pong to UFC to straight up fantasy football. Guy loves a fuckin' thrill, and he spends his money faster than he makes it. I think he cleared five hundred thousand last year."

"Jesus Christ," Anthony said under his breath, almost unable to bear the pain.

Loan Officers Wanted

Snowman was a skinny guy, mainly from doing so much coke. He wasn't much to look at, but his body had held up pretty well under the years of abuse buzzing out, not eating, and staying up late almost every night. In his early thirties, he was already balding. But Snowman was a good guy and most people liked him. He was dedicated to the job, he never bothered anyone, and mostly kept to himself at work. After work, however, he liked to go out with the guys, to joyride and party.

"Right next to him, working with that new hot Mexican chick with the nice tits, is Al. His real name is Ali, but he doesn't want his clients to know he's Middle Eastern. Now this guy is probably going to be your competition, if I know you." Al was an Iranian guy with black hair and dark intriguing eyes that were usually scheming one thing or another. He was clean cut, in good physical shape, and had a quick personality. An innate salesman, Al knew how to talk to people convincingly. He could sell loans on the job just as well as he could land chicks at the bar. He had an intense affect as he approached people which was both alarming and charismatic. Although he initially took you off guard, Al had a way of endearing people to him.

Ethan looked at Anthony squinting his eyes and nodding his head in approval, then turned back towards Al. "Fuckin' guy cleared a million last year. He gets deals from real estate agents, accountants, financial advisors, and he still cold calls to this day. The fuckin' guy is an animal. He drives the red Lamborghini Murcielago you see outside, pops more bottles at clubs than anyone I know, and has all the bitches drooling over him."

"What, are you on his nuts or something?" Anthony jostled.

"Yeah, I gave him a blowjob last night. Thanks for asking, buddy," Ethan countered.

"I'm sure you did," Anthony laughed. "So who owns this place?"

"His name is Thomas Blake, and he's filthy rich," said Ethan. "He used to be a stockbroker at some big firm, but he had a feeling Real Estate was going to blow up so he made his move. I got invited to his house for a barbeque last month, and the place must have been worth at least seven to ten million. He married some super-hot, exotic Hawaiian chick who's fuckin' over the top. I actually busted a nut last night just thinking about her," Ethan smiled. Then, becoming more serious he added, "You have to remember something dude, we're in a very competitive business. Every month a hundred new mortgage companies sprout up in California, so you have to be ruthless. 'Cause if you're not, some other guy will be, and the money that could've been yours is gonna be in his pocket. You hear me? In this business you gotta be a fuckin' killer! Got it?"

"Yeah, definitely," Anthony replied. He had made up his mind and was prepared to do whatever it took to make the kind of money all these other guys were pulling in. The entire prospect was very exciting to him. If Ethan could strike a loan that easily, then he thought he could too. It didn't look to Anthony like these other guys had anything that he didn't have, other than awesome paychecks. They had just fallen into a nice situation and used it to their advantage. Looking around the whole sales room floor, Anthony drank in the flavor of success. He knew that he was cut out for this. And he knew that this was the job opportunity he had been waiting for.

~ ELEVEN ~

THAT NIGHT, Anthony called his dad on the phone and told him he had some good news that he wanted to tell him in person. He asked his dad if he could meet him at the pizza joint. "No it's nothin' bad," Anthony reassured his dad when he asked if he should bring Anthony's mother along. "It's something that could potentially make our lives a whole lot better. You'll see dad," he said. "Just meet me at Louie's in a half hour. I'm buyin'." With that, he hung up and changed out of his dress clothes into a comfortable pair of jeans and a t-shirt. Kelly was working late that night, so Anthony would have time to meet with his dad before she got home.

Anthony arrived at the pizza joint about twenty minutes later. He was really amped up about the job and sat in the restaurant booth looking out the window at the parking lot waiting for his dad. The waitress approached his table and asked if he wanted to order anything to drink before he ordered his food. She had dark shoulder-length hair that looked as if it had been dyed black, and the name tag on her red collared shirt stated "Rochelle."

"Yeah, something to drink sounds good," Anthony said happily. "How about a pitcher of cold PBR. I'm waitin' on my old man, so please bring two glasses."

"You got it, darlin,'" the waitress replied.

As Anthony sat and waited for his father, he thought about how much he wanted to help him out financially. He thought about how hard his dad's life had been, working six days a week and barely making enough money to survive. If Anthony was able to make half of what Ethan was making, he would be able to give his mom and dad a nice vacation and a big wad of spending cash. As he sat immersed in his thoughts, he saw his dad pull into the parking lot driving his yellow cab. Anthony watched as his dad labored out of the car looking tired and smoking a cigarette. Proceeding across the parking lot, he flung the half-smoked cigarette onto the asphalt as he walked up onto the sidewalk and to the entrance.

"How you doing dad?" Anthony asked as he gave his dad hug.

"My back hurts, and my feet hurt! That's how Anthony," said his dad in a complaining tone of voice.

"Really, it's that bad, huh?" Anthony asked as they sat down at the table. "So dad," Anthony continued, half out of concern and half in jest, "When are you gonna stop smoking?"

"Never! Is that soon enough?" his father impatiently replied.

"Geez, you're in a bad mood dad. What the hell is going on?"

"It's nothing Anthony," his dad replied, feeling a bit more relaxed. "Just that your mom is telling me we have to send more money to your sister at college. And I don't know where the hell it's going to come from."

"Listen dad, stop worrying about that okay. I'll take care of Maria's college money myself. And in a couple months, I'll take care of you and mom, too." Anthony felt very strong and sure of himself as he continued, "And soon, maybe you won't have to drive that damn cab anymore."

Just then, the waitress approached their table with the pitcher of beer and two frosty beer mugs. "Here ya go, fellas. You need some more time to think about what you want order."

"Thanks dear," Anthony's dad smiled at the waitress. "Give us a few more minutes, I haven't even had time to look at the menu yet."

"Sure, no problem," the waitress said, and walked back behind the counter into the kitchen.

Returning his attention to his son, Anthony's dad exclaimed, "I see! And where are you gonna get the money to take care of us all? Are you selling dope or something?"

"No dad!" Anthony said, feeling annoyed and a little insulted. "I just got a job at Fairtex Mortgage as a loan officer, and the guys over there are making a killing. Some of them are pulling in more than a mil a year, and even Ethan is making some serious cash. So, in a couple months, hopefully I'll be able to take care of you and mom."

"Alright Anthony, just don't go getting yourself into trouble, okay. No fast money is good," his dad warned him. "Everybody who gets involved in that kind of racket ends up fucked up on dope, dead, or in prison. I seen it firsthand."

Anthony felt further annoyed by his father's comment. "Dad, can you please stop lecturing and be happy for me for once! I found a good thing, and it's gonna take care of us all for a very long time."

"Well, I'm happy to hear that Anthony, but just remember one thing! Money isn't everything in life."

"God damn it dad! Are you seriously doing this again?" Anthony argued. "I thought I said no more lectures dad! For once in my life can I do what I want?"

Anthony's dad was silent for a moment and the look of skepticism on his face softened into one of acceptance. "You know what? You're right son. You've graduated college and it's time for you to experience the real world. Just don't forget to visit your mom every once in a while, okay!"

"I will dad."

"Cheers to your new job son!"

~ TWELVE ~

ANTHONY SHOWED UP FOR WORK bright and early the next morning raring to go. He found his team in the training room and sat down next to Jessica and Hector. Looking around the large table, he noticed there were less people in the room than there had been the day before. This made him feel proud that he had come back, that he hadn't been scared off by all the brash and cocky talk from Skidmore and Lister. Taking another draw off his coffee, Anthony looked at Jessica and said, "Did you notice there's about five fewer people here today?"

"Yeah," Jessica replied. "Looks like this wasn't for them, huh?"

"I'm sure it's gonna thin out even more by the end of the week," Anthony agreed.

Cutting off their conversation, Skidmore entered the room looking like he'd been beaten with an ugly stick. Everyone in the room became suddenly very quiet and focused their entire attention on him, not wanting to be inflicted through his wrath with the same social disease he'd contracted which evidently made him talk to people like they were his cattle. In secret, however, many of them envied him. He had balls, and he said exactly what he wanted to say. He was gruff and intimidating to be sure, but he was there to make them into something they wanted to become. Rich. And the path to anything extraordinary could be brutal. At least that's what the smart guys in the room knew. The rest were just holding their breath to see how long they could last.

"Good morning everyone," Skidmore said to the group of new hires. "I had a rough night so this will be quick." He handed a stack of papers to an assisting loan officer sitting next to him.

"Everyone grab one of these sheets that are coming around. This is going to be your script. I suggest using it for one day and then making changes to fit your personality. Did everyone go over the booklet to learn about the programs we offer?" he asked the group.

Everyone in the room nodded in compliance, and replied affirmatively.

"Good!" Skidmore retorted. "You're all going to hit the phones today for three hours straight. The leads that you'll call are on your desks. Now, to make this a little fun, whoever gets the first application will get … " Brian grabbed his wallet and pulled out three crisp Benjamins, "Three hundred dollars! Now, get up off your asses and go hit the phones!"

Everyone in the room quickly gathered up their belongings and rushed off to their team manager's station, eager to land the first loan application.

Anthony, Jessica and Hector all walked over to Lister, who showed them to their own personal cubicles and had Ethan supervise. Ethan looked excited and wished them all good luck. It was nine a.m., and Anthony sat at his desk preparing to make his first call. He had never attempted to sell a loan before, and it was like diving off a ledge into a dark sea. Nonetheless, he felt confident and capable to meet the challenge as he held the piece of paper that displayed his first lead. It stated the customer's first and last name, address and phone number, the loan amount currently owed, and the lender's name and phone number. He scanned through the document making sure he had all the necessary information at the forefront of his mind. Then he picked up the phone and dialed his first number. Immediately, he heard three familiar dissonant tones followed by the familiar recorded message: "We're sorry, but the number you have dialed has been disconnected …" He hung up the phone and looked at the next customer contact sheet.

All around him, new hires examined their lead sheets, dialed numbers and received an array of responses that were less than welcoming. Busy signals, voicemails, wrong numbers, and disgruntled homeowners. A few feet away, Hector called his first lead who, upon hearing Hector's announcement that he was a mortgage loan officer, immediately hung-up on him. Other new hires were less fortunate than Hector, and were angrily cursed at by their leads. In fact, one poor guy had to take a bathroom break after his first lead yelled viciously into the phone, "I said stop calling me, asshole!"

Throughout the room, most of the new hires were yelled at by leads who had been called one too many times by loan refinancing companies, and every new hire was repeatedly rejected. Jessica had a difficult time too. Although her first lead answered the phone and was polite, he asked to be taken off the calling list. However, after a couple of wrong numbers and busy signals, Jessica finally reached another live person.

"Hi," she said, feeling both excited and nervous. "This is Jessica from Fairtex Mortgage, can I please speak with Darrell Hawkins?"

"This is him."

"Great! Mr. Hawkins, I'm calling regarding your mortgage, I wanted to know if you would be interested in lowering your rate through a refinance and ..." But before she could finish her question, the client hung-up. Feeling downtrodden but not defeated, she smiled to herself and continued dialing numbers.

It took Anthony a bit longer to get through to a live person. He felt frustrated, but somehow his angst fueled his impetus to do the job, and he kept dialing numbers until he reached his first client.

"Hello ma'am, this is Anthony Cousto. I'm calling to talk with you about refinancing your home mortgage at a lower rate."

"What?" she said. "No, I don't want to sell my home." Unfortunately, the woman was hard of hearing and had difficulty understanding who Anthony was or what he wanted.

"I said we would like to refinance your loan and lower your rate. Did you hear me ma'am? I said re-finance!"

"No thank you, there's nothing wrong with my home!" she said, and hung-up on Anthony.

It continued like this for the next three hours. Not one new hire landed a loan. The constant rejection and rid-icule put them all to the test. They had been told they could make a lot of money. They had been promised a lu-crative position in sales replete with bonuses and compa-ny trips to Vegas, but not one of them even came close to refinancing a loan with any of their leads. It was discour-aging to say the least, and a few new hires walked out the door that day never to return. But not Anthony. He was pacing himself. And he could feel a small seed burning in-side of him. It was the seed of will power and determina-tion. He knew the odds and was not weak of heart. One good refinance could put a couple grand into his pocket. And, although he was definitely motivated by the money, he had no illusions about the job being a cakewalk.

After Power Hours, Anthony, Jessica and Hector all met briefly with Ethan.

"Welcome to my world!" Ethan said laughing, knowing full well that they had all been through the ringer and not one of them had landed a loan. "Listen, don't worry about not getting your first refinance today," Ethan reassured them. "It took me about three fuckin' days of calling clients to get my own! This is hard work and sometimes it will drive you crazy. But if you stick in there, eventually you will hit it off with the right client, and 'Baam!' you got your first loan. It just takes a little time."

The three of them nodded, and Hector replied, "Yeah, I almost got one client to go with our services, but then suddenly her kids were burning dinner in the kitchen and she had to go. Damn! But I was close, Mr. Ethan."

"Not me," said Jessica. "I talked to a few people, but none of them wanted anything to do with refinancing." Feeling a bit doubtful about the job she added, "Are you sure this really works Ethan?"

"Yeah, of course it does. You're just warming up today, just getting your feet in the water. Pretty soon you'll know how to talk clients into wanting to refinance their mortgages. Trust me."

"Yeah, don't worry," Anthony added. "We gotta learn the ropes. Just make yourself laugh at those assholes that don't want your help."

Okay!" Ethan cut in, needing to get back to his own work. "I want you guys to take the rest of the afternoon off and go to the fuckin' beach! Just relax and recover and get ready for some more hell tomorrow."

<h1 style="text-align: center;">~ THIRTEEN ~</h1>

AFTER DISMISSING THE NEW HIRES, Ethan invited Anthony to come hang out with himself and some of the other seasoned loan officers later in the day. Ethan said he'd pick Anthony up at his place to take him to a restaurant where they liked to unload, and sometimes get loaded, after work. Anthony agreed, then went home feeling exhausted and took a brief nap. He awoke to the sound of Ethan knocking at the door and quickly dressed before leaving.

When Anthony and Ethan arrived at the restaurant, the three other three loan officers—Al, Snowman, and Tyson—were already seated at their table, still dressed up in their fancy work suits. Walking up to the table, Ethan cracked a smile and blurted out, "What's up my niggas? Yo, this is Anthony, my homie I been telling you guys about."

The three other loan officers chuckled at Ethan's dumb attempt to sound like he was some hip bro on the streets. As Anthony and Ethan took their seats at the table, Al looked at Anthony and said with his mildly Middle Eastern accent, "So Anthony, I have to know, does this guy really have a 4 inch dick?"

Everyone at the table busted up, except Ethan, who in a very dead-pan voice said, "Fuck you Al or Ali, or whatever the fuck they call you. Don't you have a flying carpet your supposed to be riding right about now?"

All the guys continued to laugh, until Lamar interrupted. "Anthony, I saw you making calls today at the office. Why the hell were you sweating man?"

Suddenly, Snowman stood up from the table and started to walk away, and Ethan interjected, "Yo! Where the fuck are you going?"

"I gotta take a shit," Snowman replied in a speedy voice as if it was an emergency. "You wanna come wipe my ass for me?"

"No, but Ethan's mom will be right there to do it!" Al threw in, scoring big against Ethan.

"Fuck you Al!" Ethan quickly countered.

Snowman continued to walk away from the table and went into the men's bathroom.

At this point, Lamar returned his attention to Anthony and, following up with his previous question, said "So?"

"I guess I was nervous, that's all," Anthony replied.

Taking a drink off his beer Lamar said, "That's the last thing you should be, dog." He was not being confrontational, but rather spoke in a confident but reassuring tone.

"Listen," Al cut in. "You can be whoever the fuck you want to be on the phone, do you understand?" Anthony looked confused as Al continued to explain it to him. "The leads have the borrowers current lender right?"

"Yeah, so?" Anthony responded quizzically.

"Let me tell you something," Al continued, sounding a bit more serious. "Customers don't like telemarketers. You have to make the call more of a warm lead then a cold call."

"Hmmm. Okay, that's cool. But what do you mean?" Anthony replied.

"Jesus, this guy doesn't know shit!" Al said in frustration to the group. Then, looking at his rival, he added "What kind of fuckin' friend are you Ethan?"

"Go build a bomb asshole!" Ethan replied, dismissing Al's comment.

"That's real creative, pencil dick!" Al retorted on a dime. Then he returned his attention to Anthony and said, "Cold-calling is exactly what you did today. The customer doesn't know you, doesn't know your company, so he can't trust you. Just 'cause you know their names doesn't mean these people are gonna listen to you."

"Alright," Anthony replied, feeling more curious. "So what should I do then?"

"Earn their trust!" Al exclaimed. "Let's say you're calling Mrs. Kos-kshe."

"Who the fuck is that?" Anthony quickly interjected.

"In my language, instead of calling someone a bitch we call them a Kos-kshe, which basically means *pussy stretcher* in English." At this, all the guys at the table immediately exploded in fits of laughter. "So listen," Al continued, looking at Anthony. "Let's say Mrs. Kos-kshe has her current loan with fuckin' ABC Loans, okay. This is what you would say. 'Hi Mrs. Kos-kshe, this is Brad Pitt. I'm calling from your mortgage company ABC Loans in reference to your loan with us. We wanted to offer you our new product which allows you to get a reduced interest rate of one percent%. Yes that's right Mrs. Kos-kshe, I said one percent%. I was wondering if you would be interested in hearing a little about it and see how this program can benefit you?' And that's how you get the application. Fuck that cold calling shit!"

Anthony looked confused and said, "Can you really get a one-percent interest rate on a loan?"

"What the fuck!" Al exclaimed emotionally. "Ethan, seriously, I thought this guy was your friend! Are gonna teach him anything at all? Or are you just gonna be a fuckin' shithead?"

"Your mom's gonna teach him tonight, actually!" Ethan retaliated.

Everyone laughed except Al who didn't take kindly to people joking about his mother, even if they were his good friends. "Watch yourself fucker!" he growled at Ethan. Then, looking back at Anthony, he continued his lesson. "So, Anthony, as I was saying, the 1% program is called 'Option Arm' or 'Negative Amortization.' That's the easiest sell and it makes us the majority of our money." He paused to take a sip of water, and continued, focused intensely on Anthony. "Let's say a customer takes out a loan of five hundred thousand dollars. If you do everything right and sell the shit with max fees, you're making twenty-five fuckin' grand on one loan in three or four weeks!"

Anthony was amazed by this figure, as all the other loan officers at the table nodded their heads in agreement. "Yeah, but is that a good loan?" Anthony questioned Al.

"Fuck no," Al said in a pressured whisper so as not to be overheard by anyone else in the restaurant. "The loan screws the customer in the fuckin' ass. But the lenders push us to do them 'cause they make so much money on that shit, especially if they can enforce a three-year penalty on the customer for getting out of the loan early. That's why the lenders pay us so much in rebate to do it. The loan is a fuckin' gold mine."

"What's the penalty for getting out of the loan?" Anthony asked.

"It's a lot! But don't worry about that shit! Just don't tell the customer about it. If they find out, tell them it's tax deductible and they'll shut the fuck up," Al admonished.

Just then, Snowman came back from the men's room with a faraway glossy gaze and a grin. The guys at the table all looked at him and laughed, knowing that he wasn't just taking a mammoth shit, he was doing blow. Ethan looked at Snowman laughing and said, "Look at this motherfucker, how many lines did you do, man?"

"What are you talking about, dude!" Snowman retaliated. "I just took a shit!"

"Then why you still got some blow on your nose, fucker!" Al joined in on harassing Snowman. Everyone ruptured in laughter yet again, as an attractive brunette waitress approached the table to take their order.

"Hello gentlemen. It's looks like you're all doing quite well tonight," she smiled at them. "Can I take your order?"

Looking around the table, Al said, "Order whatever you want guys, this one is on me." The guys all responded in a uproar of exaltation, and Anthony noticed other people at the restaurant looking towards their table with expressions of suspicion and judgment.

"Show off!" Lamar exclaimed to Al.

"Okay!" Ethan cheered. Then he said to the waitress, "In that case, let me get the most expensive plate of steak you have and a bottle of Crystal."

The waitress smiled and nodded as she wrote down the order. "You know what?" Lamar piped in. "I'll have the same order!"

"Make that three then!" Anthony said.

"Fuck it!" Al said. "Make it four!"

Snowman was the only one who hadn't ordered. In fact, he was the only one who hadn't even looked at a menu and didn't seem very interested in eating. The waitress looked at him and asked, "And you sir?"

"Umm, I guess I'll have the same, but hold the steak."

"Yeah, right. You only took a shit, eh?" Al looked at Snowman shaking his head in amazement while everyone laughed.

"Fuck you guys!" Snowman said to the raucous table, as the waitress walked off to the kitchen hoping they'd leave a big tip when all was said and done.

~ FOURTEEN ~

ANTHONY RETURNED TO WORK the next morning eager to hit the phones and land his first loan. He collected together the lead sheets he would need and prepared to begin calling prospective clients. Although the atmosphere was loud and busy all around him, he was not unduly distracted. Holding the lead sheets in his hand, ready to make his first call, Anthony paused for a moment and thought to himself *I really don't want to lie to my customers. But, then again, I haven't sold anything yet.* He looked around him at all the other new hires making their calls, and thought *time is wasting, and I have to make money. I mean look at the people I work with; if they can do it, then why can't I?*

In a sense, this kind of self-reassurance was nothing but a justification for Anthony. He knew something was wrong with deceiving customers, but he saw everyone else doing it and decided he would just go along with the crowd. Besides, he was motivated by the pressures to perform and to provide for his family, and he really wanted to succeed in the world and earn a living. Although he had no intentions of hurting anyone, even the best of intentions doesn't make something that's wrong right. And somewhere in the back of his mind, Anthony knew this very clearly. However, having concluded for the moment that what he was doing was okay, mainly because it was socially sanctioned at Fairtex Mortgage, Anthony picked up the phone and dialed his first number of the day.

Meanwhile, somewhere miles away in the vicinity of Irvine, Tom Bales prepared to go to work. Tom was a normal guy who held a respectable position at a decent job in corporate America. He had bought a house about ten years earlier, after getting married and having kids. But the loan repayment was high, so he was a prime target for a refinancing scheme like the one Anthony was about to sell him. Standing in his kitchen, as Tom Bales turned towards the table to polish off the last few sips of his orange juice, the phone rang.

In a hurry to get to work, Tom was a bit rushed as he said, "Hello?"

"Hi," Anthony responded. "Can I please speak with Tom Bales?"

"This is him," Tom replied, wondering who the hell was calling him this early in the morning while he was trying to get out the door.

"Mr. Bales, I'm calling you from Epson Home Loans regarding the loan you currently have with us."

Feeling irritated by this, Tom Bales said, "I already paid this month's mortgage. And I'm running late to work, so what's this about?"

"Oh yes! I do see that we have received the payment, and I won't keep you long. I'm actually calling regarding a new program that we'd like to offer you. This program allows you to get a loan rate of 1%, and you can also get some cash out or pay off credit card bills if you like.

"Really!" Tom Bales replied, feeling both delighted and surprised at how low the percentage rate was. "1% is incredible! I never heard of such a thing before. How much cash can I get?"

"We can lend you up to ninety percent% of whatever your house is worth," Anthony replied. "Do you know the current value of your house?"

His house nicely situated on a prime lot in Irvine, Bales answered, "Yes. It's been recently appraised at about seven hundred thousand."

"Okay, good," Anthony replied. "Then we can lend you up to six hundred and thirty thousand dollars. How much do you owe on the house right now Mr. Bales?"

Tom Bales paused a moment, wondering why Anthony would ask that question. "Hmmm, don't you have that information already?" he replied.

"Sure, Mr. Bales. I can look it up, but I just thought you would know and maybe save me a little time."

Feeling somewhat reassured, Tom Bales said, "Oh, okay. I owe about four hundred thousand."

"Okay, Mr. Bales. In that case, you can get up to two hundred and sixty-five thousand in cash. That's if you want it all."

Tom Bales was very pleased at this news, and thoughts of what he could do with the money raced through his head. "That would be great! I'd love to pay off a few credit cards and use some of the money to buy a new house. Maybe you can help me with that too, if this loan goes well."

"I sure can Mr. Bales," Anthony confirmed. "Now tell me, how much credit card debt are you looking to pay off? And what's the minimum total monthly payment for all your credit cards?"

"Well," Tom Bales thought about it a moment. "I have about forty grand in credit cards, and I think I pay about fifteen hundred a month on them."

"Okay sir," Anthony continued the negotiation, feeling both stalwart and sneaky. "And what's your mortgage payment?"

"Uh, it's about nineteen hundred dollars." Mr. Bales looked at his watch and felt anxious about getting to work late. But he couldn't believe the deal he was getting from Epson, so he stayed on the line.

"So you're paying a total of thirty-four hundred a month for those expenses right?" Anthony asked.

"Yes, that's right."

"Okay," Anthony began to summarize the loan refinance details. "Here's what I can do for you Mr. Bales. I can pay off your credit cards and give you about two hundred and twenty thousand in cash. Your new payment at one percent is going to be two thousand one hundred and forty dollars a month, which means I'm saving you about thirteen hundred a month, and you're getting all that cash."

Feeling very pleased with these numbers, Tom Bales said, "That sounds great, Anthony." Then he paused to think a moment and continued, "But I forgot to tell you, I do have a prepayment penalty."

"Don't worry about that Mr. Bales," Anthony replied promptly. "I'll take care of it so you don't pay anything out of your pocket."

"Let's do it then!" Bales exclaimed, heading for the car.

"Great! Now, before I let you go, can you please provide me with your social security number and date of birth?"

Nearly slipping on an orange frisbee his younger son had left in the middle of the sidewalk, Tom Bales stumbled to the side of his car with a furrowed brow and said, "Uh, don't you have that already since you're with my lender?"

"I do have it sir," Anthony quickly countered. "I just need you to verify it for your protection so no one takes out a loan in your name."

"Oh, okay Anthony. You never know who you're dealing with these days. "Goddamn scams all over the place" As he ducked into his baby blue Lexus, he gave Anthony his date of birth and Social Security number. Are you sure you can get me this deal?" he asked, feeling like it was almost too good to be true.

"Yes, definitely sir," Anthony affirmed with excitement. He could feel the electricity of landing his first loan surge like a drug through his veins. "I wouldn't offer it to you if I didn't know that I could get it for you Mr. Bales."

"Sounds great, Anthony. I've really gotta get going now. But thank you very much."

"You're welcome Mr. Bales. We'll be in touch soon. Take care."

Tom Bales hung up the phone and drove off to work feeling very happy about his improved loan situation, having no idea he'd been duped. Meanwhile, Anthony put the phone down into its holder and jumped up from his seat. He raised his right hand high in front of him to perform the ritual celebration, and brought it down fast towards his crotch yelling "Boooooom!".

Some of the new hires on the sales floor looked at him like he was crazy, but Ethan came over right away with a big grin and gave him an exuberant high-five. "Fuckin' A, dude! How much was the loan for?" Ethan asked.

Anthony smiled broadly and exclaimed "Six hundred and sixty-five thousand! And I sold the guy on the option arm!"

"You lucky son of a bitch. My first deal was just a small ass ninety grand loan. Anyway, good job homie! Welcome to the team!"

It took a lot to distract Anthony from the relative glory of that moment, but the woman who walked by right then was absolutely breathtakingly beautiful. With golden honey skin, long black hair, and curves to kill, she glanced right at Anthony with her dark brown eyes and smiled as she passed by, awakening some wild and ancient desire he hadn't felt for years.

Almost spellbound and unable to contain his interest, Anthony asked his friend, "Man, who is that?"

Ethan turned to look at who Anthony was asking about and, recognizing who it was, said "She's fine as fuck, huh?"

"Hell yeah, what's her name?" Anthony inquired.

"That's Angelina Petrone. She does real estate and loans too. But she's in a league of her own, so don't even think about it jackass. The last guy she dated was a heart surgeon, and her new boy toy is a big shot CEO."

"Who said I was interested?" Anthony quipped, feeling put off by Ethan's comment.

"Are you fuckin' kidding me? I've known you for half your life, and I can see when a hot piece of ass gets you going. But trust me, you're not gonna score her dude. Just get back to work and don't waste your time."

Anthony just stood there, rapt in the mysterious and unexpected profundity of the moment. He'd just landed his first loan—something he wanted to do that he didn't know he could do and he'd never done before—followed by seeing the most gorgeous woman he'd seen in years—someone for whom he felt an immediate and astonishing longing, though he knew he could never have her. What the hell was going on? Sometimes life was just too goddamned bewildering.

~ FIFTEEN ~

AFTER THE FIRST DEAL he sold, taking applications from clients became easy, and during the next two weeks Anthony took over fifty applications from cold calling. The next highest achieving new hire took only twenty. He was on such a roll that he started coming to work at eight in the morning and didn't leave until nine at night. Of course, there was only one way that he was able to take all those applications—a lesson he had learned early on from Al. He lied his ass off. He told clients whatever they wanted to hear just to get the application. He was such a good schmoozer that Anthony could easily convince most people to give him their confidential personal information. He learned how amazing it was what people will tell you when they think they're going to save a ton of money or get a nice, very low-interest cash advance. He was blown away that these folks would give their social security numbers to a complete stranger.

Although Anthony presented an air of humility about his instant success, inwardly he glorified in it, knowing full well how able he was to gain a client's trust in just fifteen minutes over the phone. He was smart enough to realize that there was a fine art to this whole process. He knew that if he got too friendly with them they would want to get something extra towards the end of the call, like lower fees or lower rates. So he never crossed that line, which allowed him to maintain full control over his clients. In fact, most of the time they believed everything he said, so he could do anything he wanted! For Anthony, it was like a dream in which he could control the characters, and it filled him with a sense of power and potency. And all the while he was getting rich.

Arriving at Fairtex Mortgage for another day of work, Anthony was dressed in a finely tailored, custom-made suit by Ralph Lauren. After just a few weeks he had risen to join the elite ranks of the heaviest hitters in the sales force. Although he was still considered a "newbie" by all the veteran players, he was also recognized as the most promising hew hire and, in terms of his ability to sell loans, a force to be reckoned with.

As he walked onto the sales room floor waiting for the day's meeting he noticed Angelina and made an elongated eye contact with her. He noticed her impeccable form, like an erotic, sinful angel in human form. Her breasts were full and round, and seemed to push through her blouse with their radiance. They sent magnetic, electric jolts of fiery energy through Anthony's veins, almost causing him to get tripped up on his own feet and fall on his face right there in the middle of the sales room. She was simply irrevocably and devastatingly captivating. Her beauty was audacious. It was overwhelming. Even criminal. Although Anthony hadn't exchanged words with her yet, he could sense an attraction brewing between them.

Standing in front of the group were David Konn, the manager with whom Anthony interviewed, and the owner Thomas Blake. Blake was a healthy looking man with a friendly demeanor and an aura of confidence. In his forties, he was stout, clean cut and good looking. He had dark brown hair that was graying on the sides and a tanned face that came from his habit of taking regular vacations to Rio de Janeiro, Maui, and other tropical resort towns. To the right of Konn and Blake were two very attractive female account executives—a blonde and an Asian—both sporting nice smiles and a lot of cleavage.

Konn called the meeting to order with a loud and vivacious greeting, "Good morning! Is everyone ready to make some money this month?"

A resounding "YES!" issued collectively from the sales group.

"Good!" Konn replied. "That's what I like to hear. We're on pace for another record month, so let's keep it up. Also, the contest this month is a seven-day getaway to Cabo. Now, only the top ten employees are going, so you if you want to go you better work your ass off. As always, everything will be paid for and you can bring a guest as well. Now, let me give the floor to the man that makes all of this possible!"

The sales group clapped and cheered as Blake, wearing an easy smile, took the floor. "Thank you people. It's time for my favorite part of the meeting. I'd like to go over last month's top producer and team. The top loan officer was Al, with over one hundred sixty-five thousand dollars in rev!"

The sales group all looked at Al and cheered, amazed by how much he earned.

"Congratulations Al, although we all know you're used to this by now," Blake said with a laugh. "And the top team, once again, goes to Frankie Lister who had over four hundred twenty-five thousand dollars in revenue."

Upon hearing this, Lister jumped up on a desk and performed his signature celebration for all to see, raising his open hand out high in front of him and bringing it down to his crotch with an emphatic "Boooooom!" Then he looked out at the crowd and wrinkled his face in a pompous and self-righteous expression, yelling, "That's what the fuck I'm talking about!" Most of the people in the room laughed hysterically, while some just looked at Lister like he was bat-shit crazy.

Blake himself laughed and said, "Great job Frankie, but please get down from the desk."

"Sorry 'bout that boss," Lister replied. "I just got a little excited." Then he proceeded to climb down from the desk and resumed his authoritative stance, with arms akimbo and a stern expression on his face.

"That's okay Frankie," Blake added. "I just don't want you to scare off all the great new talent we have here at our meeting! On that note," Blake continued, looking down at a sheet of paper, "I'd like to recognize someone who has only worked here for a month, but has made a great start. That's Anthony Cousto, with over sixteen loans submitted so far."

Everyone in the room clapped for Anthony, but especially his team of Ethan, Al, Lamar, and Snowman who also whistled and hooted rambunctiously while calling out epithets intended to embarrass him.

As everyone settled down, Blake continued. "Now, please give all of your attention to Lauren Ganes and Lillian Chang. They're the account executives for Belmont Wholesale and their company has some of the best rates and guidelines around the industry. So, please listen carefully."

Of course, no one really liked to listen to some outside group give a speech about shit they were selling. But Ethan sure as hell didn't mind looking at them. As they began their presentation, he looked to Anthony and said under his breath, "Damn, those chicks are fuckin' hot! I'd like about five minutes in a dark room with both of them."

"Yeah, I'm sure you would," Anthony snickered. However, being newer than Ethan, he was a little more interested in understanding what these account representatives were actually talking about. "So, all we do is call these girls to get rates, right?" he asked Ethan.

"No, that's not all," Ethan explained to him. "These reps can help you make money or not. They're just as shady as we are. Let's say you can't qualify someone, all you have to do is call one of these reps and she'll help you find a way to get around the problem and still get the client approved. Remember, they make money off the business we give them. So, most of the time, they'll do whatever it takes. Why do you think we get free lunches all the fuckin' time? So they can come here and go over deals with us?" Ethan paused, then continued with a sardonic smile. "Plus, they're fine as fuck. I think four of the guys in our office fucked the blonde, and Snowman fucked the Asian in the bathroom a week ago."

Anthony was impressed by how helpful these young ladies were, both in the realm of business and pleasure. He listened attentively as Ethan continued.

"They make serious money too. Most of them pull six figures easy, and some in the millions. Everyone wants to retire off this shit, man!" Licking his chops, he added, "Fuck, that Asian bitch is hot!"

"Don't you ever stop?" Anthony asked his friend.

Ethan smiled and exclaimed, "Nope!"

~ SIXTEEN ~

LISTER'S SALES TEAM continued to have another exemplary month. That is, everyone but Ethan. For some reason, ever since Anthony had joined the team Ethan had been in a serious slump. Maybe it was that Ethan secretly felt threatened by Anthony's superior sales prowess. And maybe it was just a coincidence. Because every salesman, at one point or another, can't sell a cold cup of lemonade to a thirsty millionaire in the desert. That's just how it was. Although Al seemed to have proved that theory wrong with his continual ability to exceed his own marks. However, maybe Al was just the exception to the rule. At any rate, Ethan's normally buoyant mood had been punched through with fits of exasperation and angst at failing to land one single loan all month long, and everyone on his sales team had noticed. So they decided to take him out for lunch at a nearby brewery and try to lighten his mood.

Although Al's conversation style was slick as pigeon shit on a sidewalk with his clients, he actually abandoned all tact with his friends. "So," he asked Ethan after taking a big slug off his beer, "when are you gonna close a fuckin' loan, turd?"

Ethan, lacking the will to fight at this point, just looked down shaking his head, and said, "I don't know."

Then he added, "Even Tanya, the girl I've been seeing, is trippin'. I think she's gonna leave me for some fuckin' rich guy now that I'm not making any money this month."

"She's a slut, man," Snowman interjected. "I told you at the beginning. She was giving you head at the club, what do you think she's an angel?"

"Yeah, my friend. She's a god damn gold-digger, homie. She's probably the reason you haven't closed a loan." Al actually looked concerned about Ethan for once.

Shattering the momentary thoughtfulness at the table, Lamar blurted out, "I fucked her, dude!"

While everyone else laughed uproariously, Ethan only became more contorted in his head and agonized in his heart. "What!" he said. "Fuck you Lamar! You didn't fuck my girlfriend!"

"Yeah I did, man," Lamar retorted. "I just never told you 'cause you were all sprung over her. But now that she's doin' you dirty, I might as well tell you."

"Fuckin' shit, man!" Ethan spat at the table. "When did you fuck her?"

"Right before you hooked up with her," Lamar replied. "She used to meet me in the parking lot and give me head at lunch. So, one time I just banged her in the car."

Like a gnarly crowd of onlookers at a wrestling match, all the guys at the table howled and heckled Ethan. "Fuck bro," Ethan protested. "She told me she loved me!"

"He loved her," Al cajoled Ethan, laughing so hard he nearly pissed his pants. "I can't take this anymore. Oh my god Ethan, you're such a fuckin' idiot!"

"Sorry brother," Lamar, in a failed attempt, tried to reassure Ethan. "But she's a ho fo sho."

No one said anything for a minute or so, which allowed Ethan to shake off the shock. Then Snowman offered, "You know what you need Ethan?"

"No, what?" Ethan replied, looking like someone had spiked his beer with rat poison.

"You need to fuckin' move on dude! We're gonna take you out tonight and get you wasted and then fucked by some hot ass chick. And tomorrow," Snowman paused to sniff at his raw nostril, "you can tell that bitch it's over, okay!"

Feeling forlorn and defeated, but happy to at least have his friends, Ethan agreed saying, "I'm down for that, but Anthony has to come with us."

Everyone immediately looked at Anthony. He got one of those expressions on his face that people get when they are caught completely off guard and put on the spot. Then he said in an apologetic tone, "I can't go tonight, I'm busy with Kelly."

"Really? You're busy with Kelly every fuckin' night!" Ethan complained. Then he asked, "What the hell do you have to do with her tonight?"

Anthony felt a little embarrassed being called out like that in front of the guys. So he said, a little more defensively this time, "We're going to the movies. I promised I'd take her."

"You're such a pussy!" Ethan chastised. "Why don't you take her out on Sunday?" Then, inflecting his voice mockingly and smiling he added, "Anyways, your other girlfriend, Angelina, will be there." Ethan knew he'd get under Anthony's skin with that last comment. Evidently, he got under the skin of all the other guys too, as they all looked like a bunch of slackjaws staring at Anthony like he was nuts.

"What!" Al exclaimed. "I told you before, bro. You got no chance with her! I tried to hit that and she even turned me down."

Anthony downplayed the whole scene, "Who said I want her anyway?" He took a slow, casual sip off his beer and added, "And even if I did, I'm married. So what's the point?"

"Yeah," Lamar chimed in. "That girl is dangerous! Stay the fuck anyway from her Anthony."

Then Snowman looked at Anthony and said, "So, are you coming with us tonight or not?"

Anthony thought about it for a moment and said, "Alright, but just this once, okay?"

"Yeah man," Lamar said smiling. "Just this once."

<h2 style="text-align:center">~ SEVENTEEN ~</h2>

KELLY WASN'T VERY HAPPY with Anthony going out on a weeknight with the guys at the office without her, especially to some upscale, ritzy club. But she tolerated it. She felt a little more intimidated when Al came to the apartment to get Anthony driving his red Lamborghini. "Don't have too much fun tonight, Anthony! And come home before midnight, okay?" she entreated him before he left.

"You know I will," he replied. Kelly looked at Anthony sideways, with slanted eyes. "I mean I'll come home before midnight and I won't have too much fun! Don't worry sweetheart, it's just a little outing with the guys," he reassured her. "And it's just this once. They begged me to go. Ethan's getting fucked over by his girlfriend, so we all wanted to cheer him up."

"Really, I didn't know Ethan had a girlfriend," Kelly replied. "Must not have been for long."

"Yeah, but for Ethan dating someone over a month is a big deal," Anthony said. "You know how he's constantly striking out with the ladies."

Kelly laughed, and teased him, "Yes, quite the opposite from his good-looking friend Anthony Cousto, huh?" She stroked the back of his hair and said, "'Cause you're always hittin' grand slams with me." She kissed him on the neck and said, "Have a good time with your friends Anthony. Just remember me when you're looking at all the pretty ladies on the dance floor."

Anthony dismissed Kelly's comment, saying "I only have eyes for you, baby. See you in a couple hours." Then he kissed her and walked out the door to the car where Al was waiting for him.

"Yo, man. What took you so long Anthony?" Al asked with a glimmer in his eyes. His car was a spectacular piece of work, and blasted Snoop Dogg on the sound system as Anthony reclined into the plush leather seat.

"Damn man," Anthony said. "Where'd you get this baby?"

"Oh, I have a friend who works at the dealer down in Newport Beach," Al replied revving up the engine. "He cut me a really good deal. Although shit," Al chortled, "who needs a good deal when you're cleaning up every day at Fairtex Mortgage!" He raised his hand to give Anthony a casual high-five, then added, "I hear you're doing very well yourself, my man."

"Yeah, so far so good," Anthony replied. "But I guess we gotta get Ethan back on track, eh?"

"Yeah, don't worry about Ethan my friend. He's not bad at sales, but he fluctuates. He'll come back sooner or later, probably once he ditches that loose cunt he's been fucking."

"Yeah," Anthony said, "maybe we can help him with that tonight, eh?"

"That's the idea, Anthony."

A few minutes later, Anthony and Al arrived at the club. As always, Al attracted a lot of attention with his red Lamborghini. Al greeted the doorman who knew him well and let him and Anthony in without asking for ID or requesting the typical cover charge. The inside of the club was palatial, with high ceilings and multiple levels. Along one whole side of the club, opposite the bar, was a tinted glass wall behind which beautiful naked dancers undulated sinuously like serpents in love. Anthony and Al walked through the crowd to a table in the VIP section of the bar where Ethan, Snowman and Lamar sat with their drinks waiting for them. As they walked, the waitresses and other club staff nodded knowingly at Al as he was a regular who threw down large sums of cash at their establishment on a weekly basis. Anthony wasn't accustomed to this kind of public attention or acknowledgment, and it evoked a strange feeling of importance in him, along with a mild feeling of discomfort.

Arriving at the table, the guys were happy to see Anthony and Al. They immediately called the waitress over who poured them a round of shots. Al raised his glass and toasted the group, "This is to a crazy fuckin' night!" The table replied in kind, and the waitress took their drink orders.

Looking around, Anthony was impressed by the magnitude of the club. Although he and Kelly liked to go out drinking and dancing sometimes, they'd never gone to a club as swank as this one. The crowd appeared to be very affluent and the atmosphere was somewhat eccentric to him. Anthony wasn't used to having money or hanging out with rich guys. Just a couple of months before, he'd been an impecunious student. And growing up, he and his family were among the working poor. The cultural status of the club was a new social experience for him, and it was very stimulating.

The guys all razzed Ethan about needing to get laid that night. Then, after tossing back a few drinks, they all took off towards the dance floor to test their luck with the ladies, leaving Anthony alone at the table. Feeling a bit inebriated and curious about the terrain of the bar, Anthony got up from the table and began walking around. Sauntering past the main area of the club, he continued down a short hallway and entered a smaller room in which a lime colored light suffused the air and the music was more mellow. Inside, couples lounged on comfortable chairs and smoked hookahs while a ventilation system drew all the smoke up and out of the club. Anthony guessed this was the smoking room. Since he didn't smoke, he just smiled at the people, then resumed walking through the club.

Striding back towards the main club floor, he veered right up a long flight of stairs which led to a balcony walkway overlooking the main portion of the club. There was another bar at the end of the walkway and Anthony strolled down towards it with his drink in hand. He paused on the bar stool and finished his drink, then ordered another from the bartender. There was a smaller dance floor on this level with a few less people, so he sat with his drink and watched the people dance while taking in the vibe of the place. As he sat in a reverie of strobe lights and loud, bassy music, entranced by the newness and the unusualness of his surroundings, he felt a hand gently rest upon his shoulder. He turned to look and saw that it was Angelina from the office.

"Hi," she said, smiling. "You're Anthony right?"

"Yes I am," Anthony replied.

Then she added, "I just wanted to say good job on submitting all those loans. I mean, I don't think anyone has ever submitted that many in their first month."

"Well, thanks. Aren't you Angelina?"

"Yeah, that's me," she said with a little laugh.

"Well, I've heard a lot about you," Anthony said smiling.

"Oh yeah?" she giggled again. "And what's that?"

"Oh, nothing bad at all. I was just told you do very good at the company," Anthony reassured her.

"Oh really, and who told you that?" Angelina questioned.

"Mainly Ethan," said Anthony. "He's my old friend. He helped me get the job."

"I see. Well, it's a good thing for him that you're doing so well or he might have looked bad, huh?" she teased him. Then, looking around a little, she added "So, is this your first time here?"

"Yeah, it is," Anthony said as he took another sip of his drink. The sight of Ethan dancing wildly with a hot young babe in a yellow go go skirt on the dance floor distracted him for a moment, and he smiled to himself. Then he returned his attention to Angelina and asked, "Do you come here a lot?"

"No, not really," Angelina replied. "I usually try to go to places where mortgage people aren't the majority, but nowadays it's kind of hard."

"And what's wrong with mortgage people?" Anthony teased.

"Nothing really," Angelina laughed. "It's just that I'm around them all day long, talking about the same things. And a little change is nice every once in a while, you know?"

"I hear you," Anthony agreed.

Just then, a man Anthony hadn't seen before approached them and said to Angelina, "You ready to get out of this dump?"

"Hi baby," Angelina said affectionately to the man. "I was just saying 'hi' to Anthony. He started working at the office last month." Then she turned to Anthony and said, "This is my boyfriend Brandon."

Brandon chewed gum like a used car salesman and avoided eye contact with Anthony. Even so, Anthony extended his hand to give him a handshake and introduced himself. However, Brandon ignored this gesture and, sardonically dissing Anthony, said impassively, "Nice to meet you Erika, but we gotta go. My Jet is waiting to take us to New York for the weekend. You ready to go, babe?"

"Yeah, sure hun. Let's go," Angelina said to Brandon. Then she turned back to Anthony and said, "It was nice to finally meet you Anthony. I'll see you around the office."

"Same here," Anthony said, feeling a little put off by Angelina's asshole boyfriend, but glad he'd run into Angelina.

Angelina and Brandon walked off and Anthony just shook his head, wondering why such a nice girl would hook up with such a thoughtless prick.

"Fuck that trust fund bitch!" Anthony heard a voice say. He turned to see Ethan, very drunk and stumbling more than standing beside him. "Her piece of shit boyfriend only has money 'cause his dad died and left the company to him," Ethan added. Then he attempted to take another swallow of his already empty drink and, upon realizing that he'd already killed it, slammed the glass down loudly on the table. "You see what god damn money gets you?" Ethan implored his friend.

"Yeah, I do." Anthony replied. "Hey, what happened to that sexy girl you were just dancing with?"

"Oh, she said she had to go to the bathroom and never came back. Fuck that bitch too," Ethan said drunkenly, slurring his words. Then, putting his arm around Anthony he added, "Let's go find the guys."

Anthony and Ethan clamored down the stairs to the main part of the club, Anthony leading the way and keeping Ethan from falling and breaking his neck. Once they got to the bottom of the stairs, Ethan broke off from Anthony and took the lead, saying "C'mon, man. Follow me. I know where those fools are." Anthony followed

Ethan to the back of the club where the music was less loud and the lights were dim. Anthony thought Ethan was either lost or just fucking with him until they came to a door which Ethan knocked on. Standing there, they both heard the other guys inside laughing and whoopin' it up.

Ethan opened the door and they saw all the other guys having their own private party with a few girls from the club. The guys were all sitting at a nice table while the girls moved around the room, talking and dancing. Anthony saw lines of white powder on the table and a rolled up hundred dollar bill. As it occurred to him what was going on, Al cut in saying, "Where the fuck have you guys been?"

"At the upstairs bar," Anthony answered.

"Yeah," Ethan chimed in. "Anthony was talking to Angelina!"

"What! That's my boy!" Lamar bellowed. Then he put the rolled up dollar bill to his nose and snorted a line of cocaine from the table.

Snowman turned his attention to Anthony and said, "You want some?"

"Nah," Anthony muttered. "I'm cool."

"Come on dog," Snowman prodded him. "You're part of the crew now, so take one hit at least. This shit is fuckin' good!"

Anthony felt anxious at the proposition of doing coke. He was already a little bit drunk and he didn't want to get wasted and be out late. He knew that would only piss off Kelly. "Nah man, that's okay," he replied. "I'll take a rain check this time."

"What the fuck Anthony!" Ethan protested. "Just take one god damn hit, it's not gonna kill you." Continuing in a drunken and mocking tone he said, "And I promise Kelly won't find out!"

"You know, he's right Anthony," Al joined in, putting the pressure on him. "You're part of the crew now, so at least do one line, man."

The guys waited to see how Anthony would respond. It was beginning to get late and their eyes were all bloodshot and blurry as they looked at Anthony, almost like kids pleading with their parents.

"Alright," Anthony said. "What the fuck! Give me a line of that shit!"

Snowman made a fresh line for Anthony and handed him the rolled up hundred dollar bill. Anthony looked briefly at Ethan as if through a haze of melancholy, then bent his head down and sniffed the line of coke up into his bloodstream.

"That's my boy!" Ethan said. "How was it?"

"Good." Anthony replied, coughing a little and nodding his head.

"Well, do another one," Ethan encouraged him.

Caught up in the moment, Anthony acquiesced and snorted up another line. The lights swirled and the music metamorphosed into liquid pellets of bliss dancing on his brain, as he sat back in his chair and felt the rush like an ecstatic hum filling his body with life.

The guys all smiled at him, and Al spoke out to the ladies, "Girls, come over and meet Anthony!"

~ EIGHTEEN ~

THE NEXT DAY AT WORK, Anthony sat at his desk late in the afternoon reviewing paperwork. Ethan approached him, still a bit hung over, and said, "God damn Anthony, you look about as bad as I feel. What the hell happened?"

Anthony was so occupied he hadn't even noticed Ethan until he started talking. He looked up from his desk with an expression of exasperation and said, "Remember that first deal I sold for six hundred and sixty-five thousand dollars?"

"Yeah, you lucky son of a bitch!" Ethan said. "I remember."

Anthony frowned and said, "Well, I just got a call from my processor and she told me it didn't get approved 'because the guy doesn't make enough money." After pausing a moment he continued, "So, what the fuck am I supposed to do now?"

"Let me see the W-2," Ethan replied. Anthony handed Mr. Bales' W-2 to Ethan and he looked it over. "Alright," Ethan continued, working out the plan in his head. "So, the guy makes a hundred and ten thousand a year. What does he need to make for the deal to go through?"

"I think around a hundred and forty thousand," Anthony replied.

"Okay," Ethan said, nodding his head confidently. "Don't fuckin' worry. It's not dead at all. You might have to re-submit it to another lender now, but it's still gonna get done." He smiled at Anthony and added, "Take off work a little early today and go to an arts and crafts store. Buy a glue stick and an X-ACTO knife, then meet me back here tonight at ten o'clock." He smiled mischievously and said, "I have a few things I need to teach you."

"Alright," Anthony said, wondering what the hell Ethan had up his sleeve. "As long as it's not some secret, demented sexual fantasy you want me in on with your crazy ass girlfriend!"

Ethan laughed and walked off shaking his head, saying, "Just get the shit and meet me here as planned."

Anthony did as Ethan had requested. He had no idea what the fuck Ethan was up to, but he trusted him. Ethan had gotten him the job and now, hopefully, he was going to help him to overcome his first big hurdle. If it meant he'd have to go to the arts and crafts store first, he'd just do it. That night, Anthony didn't tell Kelly exactly why he was going back to work; he just said there was a major issue with one of his clients that Ethan was going to help him with. At this point, Kelly was getting more used to Anthony working long hours and she usually understood. As long as she got regular nookie and a couple dates a week with him, she was happy. She'd been very supportive of his new job venture and he appreciated it. But, in truth, he didn't know how lucky he was.

That night, Kelly made a nice, fragrant pot roast with fresh carrots, peas and potatoes. They dined in candlelight while listening to Frankie Sinatra on the radio. He'd always been one of Kelly's favorite singers. At nine forty five p.m., Anthony jumped up from the table, gave Kelly a big kiss, and drove back to work.

Before he got out of his car, Anthony grabbed the X-ACTO knife and the glue stick and put them in his brief case. He wasn't sure exactly what he'd be using them for, but he didn't want to look like an idiot carrying some arts and crafts shit that he didn't even want through the office. He got out of the car and walked to the front entrance. He'd never been there this late and thought it would just be Ethan and himself, but once he walked inside he saw that there were five other loan officers still working as well. Walking across the sales room floor he noticed the mood was more serious, even solemn at this late hour. He passed by one of the loan officers who was working quietly by himself. The loan officer was holding an official document up to a translucent pane of glass that had a bright yellow light behind it. He had superimposed another document over top of the first and was situating it perfectly so that he could forge a client's signature onto the top document. Anthony looked at the loan officer as he walked by him and said, "hello." The loan officer simply nodded silently to Anthony in a matter-of-fact manner and resumed his work.

Anthony continued across the sales room floor carrying his brief case. He looked professional, as always, but felt secretive. Not secretive in a sophisticated way, but in a dumb way like he was some stupid kid at school getting ready to play a prank on the teacher with his buddy. He saw Ethan and walked over to his cubicle. Ethan saw him as he approached and nodded. "Why are people here so late?" Anthony asked Ethan when he got close enough to speak in a low tone. "I thought the office closed at nine."

"It does," Ethan concurred. "But after hours we get the shady deals approved." He smiled and added, "Welcome to the world of magic sticking. Did you get the stuff?"

Anthony pulled the glue stick and the X-ACTO knife out of his brief case and placed it on Ethan's desk with a look of confusion. "Here it is. What the fuck do we need this shit for?"

"I'll show you," Ethan replied. "Give me the customer's W-2s." Anthony retrieved those from his brief case and placed them on Ethan's desk as well. "Did you make the extra copies?" Ethan asked, as he looked through them.

"Yeah, it's all there," Anthony replied. "So are you gonna show me what the hell you're up to here?"

Ethan remained silent, absorbed in his work as Anthony watched him study Mr. Bales' 2004 W-2. Having looked through all the vital information, Ethan picked up the X-ACTO knife. In the box entitled "Wages, tips, and other compensation" the sum of $110,841.87 was printed. Ethan opened the X-ACTO knife and very carefully cut out the "4" in this sum. He then opened up the glue stick and pasted a little on the back of the tiny piece of paper with the "4" on it. Then he picked up another copy of Mr. Bales' W-2 and pasted the "4" on top of the income earned amount, changing it to $140,841.87.

"See what I'm talkin' about?" Ethan asked Anthony. "I think Mr. Bales just earned enough last year to qualify for the re-fi!"

Anthony watched, half in horror and half in astonishment, as Ethan then took the X-ACTO knife and cut out a "7" from the first W-2 and pasted it on the second W-2 in the box marked "Federal income tax withheld," changing the amount displayed from $20,568.34 to $27,568.34.

"And now," Ethan bragged, "Mr. Bales' income taxes are in synch with his earnings. Voila! Here's your new W-2." Ethan smiled like a veritable bank robber who'd just cracked the code on a safe. "Boom, bitch! You see that shit? Now your loan's gonna get approved."

"What the fuck!" Anthony protested. "We can't do that. The lender will find out."

"No they won't, dude," Ethan reassured him. "That's why I said to just submit it to a new lender. Besides, the lenders barely even verify shit anymore. Maybe one out of twenty loans, so you're good homie!"

"Man, Ethan, you sure we're not gonna get in trouble for this?" Anthony implored, beginning to sweat.

"Yeah, I'm sure. Everybody does it, what the fuck do you think those shitheads are doing over there? Anyways, I told you already, if you don't do it someone else will. You want that?" Ethan waited for Anthony to answer. When he didn't, Ethan continued, "That's what I thought. Now come on and watch what I do." Ethan got up from behind his desk and walked over to the Xerox machine with Anthony following him. He opened the lid and placed the W-2 face down on the screen, then closed the top.

"Now you gotta make a copy of it. But make sure it gets copied in a lighter shade so none of the lines show up." Ethan picked up the fresh copy that the machine had just spit out and walked with Anthony back to his desk. "Here you go," he said, handing the new W-2 to Anthony. "Give this to your processor tomorrow and tell her to resubmit it."

Anthony studied the W-2, feeling hesitant about the whole thing. "I can still see the lines!" he nearly yelled when he spotted them on the form.

Ethan took the W-2 back and looked at it. "Don't worry," he said. "Here's the last thing you do." He took the X-ACTO knife and scratched off the lines around the new numbers. "Now just make another copy and we're done."

After making a new copy of the W-2, Anthony came back and said, "So you're telling me everybody does this shit?"

"Yeah, they do," Ethan confirmed. "The way the lenders see it, the homeowners are all just gonna refinance in eight months anyway. So who fuckin' cares, right?"

Anthony and Ethan both looked at the final copy of the altered W-2. "Damn, this shit looks clean!" Ethan exclaimed. All the lines around the numbers that had been glued on the dummy copy were gone, and the new copy looked almost as good as an original.

"Yeah," Anthony agreed. "This shit looks good."

"Yeah, I know it does," Ethan said. "But the W-2's are the easy ones to do. All you had to do with that one is make everything based off a hundred-and-forty-grand salary. The pay stubs are a little more tricky. But don't worry, you'll pick it up quickly." Ethan chuckled gleefully to himself as he collected the pay stubs belonging to a few clients he was working on. "Now remember, you can do this shit with anything: tax returns, credit reports, pensions, and even bank statements. Now let me show you pay stubs!"

Anthony watched as Ethan continued to work. That night he learned the most valuable thing you could possibly learn in mortgage. How to "magic stick," as they called it. From that moment on, Anthony never lost a loan because he couldn't get it approved. Magic sticking was the key to his success, and it was more of an art form to him than just glue and an X-ACTO knife. In fact, it became a regular way of doing business.

~ NINETEEN ~

THE NEXT WEEKEND, Anthony was invited over to Al's place to celebrate the completion of his first loan. Because he was already tight with Ethan, and because he was selling the hell out of the loans, he'd become a regular member of their group. And although, technically speaking, Ethan had given him a big boost, it was a status that Anthony felt he'd earned through his own sweat and blood working long, hard hours. While Kelly wasn't entirely comfortable with Anthony hanging out with these guys, it was something she understood and tolerated. Of course, Anthony hadn't told her about the drugs or the girls. But, then again, what guy in his right mind would? Those were just additional perks that came along with the territory of earning big bucks. And it wasn't like he planned on squandering away all his money when it came. He remained committed to helping out his folks and paying for his sister's college expenses like he'd promised he would. And that made him feel very good about himself.

Anthony was beginning to ride the wave of success, and hanging out with the guys was just another way of celebrating it. If he didn't, they'd look at him like an outsider, and his morale at work might drop. Then again, Anthony had never before hung out in the VIP section of cush clubs or spent afternoons in the homes of millionaires, so it was all quite novel and entertaining to him to say the least. Kelly had questioned why he never brought her along on any of his lavish adventures with the guys, and he had told her the truth, that they were all single dudes who became wicked and offensive to most sensible women when they partied. In essence, he was saving her the hassle of dealing with a bunch of shit she'd probably rather not encounter now that she'd graduated from college.

It was a fine, sunny Saturday afternoon as Anthony drove over to Al's. He knew he was getting closer because the homes were growing in size and opulence. Parking on the side of the street, Anthony checked the address in his phone to make sure it matched the one on Al's gated mansion. He got out of the car and called Al on the telecom at the entrance to the driveway so that he could get inside. Al buzzed him in, and Anthony entered the grand estate which was luxuriously landscaped with flower gardens and exotic bushes. The place was a two-story brick and wood combo done in a very appealing art deco style. It donned a four car garage, vaulted ceilings, and a swimming pool and hot tub in the back. Al's red Lamborghini Murcielago was parked outside, while his silver Mercedes-Benz, white Range Rover, and black convertible Porsche were kept inside the garage.

Feeling excited and a bit intimidated by the grand display of wealth, Anthony approached the front door and rang the bell. As if he was still living in the college dormitory, he heard a cacophony of male voices yell for him to come in, so he did.

Walking through the front area, Anthony followed the voices around the corner and past a cute young blonde who was cleaning in the kitchen. He filed past a few large carpeted rooms that were empty except for random cardboard boxes here and there, to the spacious entertainment room which opened up with a high ceiling and skylight. There Ethan, Al, Snowman, Lamar, and Hector sat watching a ping-pong match on a sixty-five-inch flat screen TV mounted on the wall. Evidently this room was the center point of action in Al's mansion home. Through large bay windows, Anthony saw a sprawling beautiful blue spiral swimming pool in the backyard and a nice vista of the California hills beyond. The guys were all sitting on leather couches, drinking beer, and yelling at whatever was happening on the TV. There were a few lines of cocaine on the table, alongside the infamous hundred dollar bill. As soon as the guys saw Anthony, they all cheered his having popped his cherry by completing his first loan. Anthony raised his right hand, and performed the victory ritual bringing his hand down to his crotch and yelling "Boooooom!"

Al got up from the black leather couch and put his arm around Anthony, saying, "Congratulations on closing your first loan! You want a drink?"

"Sure!" Anthony replied.

Al called out to the blonde in the other room, "Baby, can you please get Anthony a beer?"

"Sure honey!" she called out in response. "I'll bring it right over."

"Thank you," Anthony said.

"Come on man," Al encouraged Anthony. "Sit down and get comfortable. Make yourself at home!"

Anthony sat down next to Ethan, who asked him "So, which loan did you close?"

As the blonde girl came over and gave Anthony his beer, he replied to Ethan, "The one you helped me magic stick."

"Fuck yeah!" Ethan exclaimed. "I told you that shit would work! How much did you make on that?"

"I charged him max!" Anthony smiled, slugging down his beer.

"That a boy!" Snowman threw in. "How much was that?"

"Around, thirty-three thousand. So, I get fourteen of that. And I gave him the Option Arm too."

"Another one bites the dust!" Lamar exclaimed.

"Yeah, that's good shit," Al said looking at the TV. "But the game's back on Anthony, and we all got a lot of money on this muthafucka!"

Anthony looked toward the TV and was perplexed. He turned to Hector and asked under his breath, "Why the fuck are we watching ping-pong?"

"'Cause they all bet on the game, homie," Hector replied.

"Really? Are you serious?"

"Yep!" Hector confirmed. "Al bet thirty grand on the Chinese guy and Lamar has twenty on him. Snowman and Ethan both have fifteen on the Russian guy. That's why they're so into the game."

"That's fuckin' crazy!" Anthony muttered.

Suddenly, Al and Lamar jumped up and down with excitement because the Chinese guy just scored another point.

"Oh my god!" Al said to Lamar. "One more fuckin' point! C'mon you motherfucker. You can do this!" Al hollered at the TV.

On his next serve, the Chinese guy scored the winning point and Al and Lamar went crazy, howling and high-fiving each other as if they were a couple of Chinese fans themselves. Ethan and Snowman, on the other hand, just slunk back to the couch and cursed angrily at both the Chinese and the Russian players, neither of whom would ever hear them.

"Man, that was so close," Lamar said to Al. "I can't believe he came back!"

"I know dog! That was some fuckin' crazy shit!" Al agreed.

"Fuck that!" Snowman complained. "Who's playing next?"

Ethan grabbed the newspaper off an end table to see. "Looks like it's Japan versus South Korea."

Snowman pulled his cell phone out of his pocket to make a call. "Wussup Joe! Yo, what's the odds on the next game?" After pausing a second he said, "Alright, I'll do another fifteen grand on Japan. Ethan, you betting?"

"Yeah, give me the phone!" Ethan shouted.

Snowman threw the phone to Ethan, who barked into it, "Joe! Let me get the same bet too. Cool. Thanks."

"Man! You guys are fuckin' nuts!" Anthony said out loud shaking his head. "Seriously!"

"Fuck yeah we are," Al said. "But life's a risk carnal! Remember, we don't fake it, we just take it!"

At that, Snowman offered some blow to Anthony who quickly snorted up two lines. The rest of that day and the whole year long Anthony learned how to party with the high rollers. Ethan and Al and the others had only been his initial induction into this new extravagant lifestyle. After that Anthony took the ball and ran.

~ TWENTY ~

A YEAR LATER, to celebrate his newfound success, Anthony bought his first new car, a shiny black Porsche 911 twin turbo with leather interiors, power steering and a sunroof. At work he was known as "The Killer Kong" because he landed so many loans, even threatening to pass up Al. He was one of the most well-respected loan officers and had his own VIP parking spot. He was on an amazing roll, and nothing was going to stop him. His first year at Fairtex Mortgage he made more than four hundred thousand dollars, which enabled him to pay off all his credit cards and student loans, make a serious dent in his parent's mortgage, and fund his sister Maria's college tuition. He even bought Kelly an eighty-thousand-dollar shiny blue BMW convertible which they drove up the coast on weekends to Big Sur and Monterey Bay. For Christ's sake, his very first year on the job he went to the Super bowl game in Houston on an all-expense-paid trip courtesy of the company. Who the fuck could say they did all that in their first year at any job?

In terms of success, Anthony couldn't have been any happier. As it turned out, he was making more money than all three of his college buddies combined. John dropped out of Law School and even Steve quit his job so they could take a stab at the mortgage business. Anthony was making so much money that one of the drawers in his desk at work had nothing in it but checks he hadn't had the time to deposit. It was right next to the drawer in which he kept all his magic sticking supplies: W-2's, paystubs, 401k's, pension income statements, glue stick, and most importantly, the X-ACTO knife.

In order to make so much money, Anthony lied, cheated, deceived and completely misled his clients, as well as the banks. Magic sticking was a good term for what he did, because it involved creating a fantasy world through which he enchanted his clients before destroying their dreams—at which point he used the wreckage and ashes of their failed endeavors to build his own empire. But, over time, this kind of malicious business activity became a normal routine and did not disturb his conscience. He was so high on the bliss of his success, not to mention the cocaine, that he'd become numb to the reality of how badly he was hurting his clients through manipulating and completely ruining their financial stability and, thus, their rank and reputation.

For once in his life, Anthony had attained a position of authority and power in which he was duly respected for his ability to accomplish a highly valued goal: sales. And he was handsomely rewarded for it through massive financial profits. Within just one year of his life, he had virtually sprung up from rags to riches. He was on a mission to become a multimillionaire by the time he was thirty, and he felt like nothing in the world could stop him.

~ TWENTY-ONE ~

ANTHONY SAT AT HIS DESK working late into the night. He was doing the dirty "after hours" task of magic sticking. Although, in actuality, it was a very simple process; it never failed to thrill him. It was kind of like playing God, how in just a few minutes he could increase a client's bank account from three thousand dollars to thirteen thousand or, at least in his own version of virtual reality. The banks never questioned him, and his clients never seemed to find out what he had done to their paperwork. He was living in his own little private secret world in which he could make the wheels of commerce turn to his exact specifications. The whole process was simply ingenious.

As he sat absorbed in his work, glue stick and X-ACTO knife upon the desk amidst piles of scattered bank statements and W-2s, he heard a knock upon his office door. "Come in," Anthony called out.

The door swung slowly open and in walked Angelina. She looked a bit tired, Anthony thought, but still as beautiful and mesmerizing as ever. "Oh, hi! What are you doing here so late?" Anthony asked her, quite surprised that she had come to see him.

Her hand curled lingeringly around the doorknob, as if she needed to establish her entrance or remind herself that she had really come. She smiled shyly and looked around Anthony's office, before answering, "Oh, the same thing as you are probably. Just finishing up work." She moved languidly towards the chair in front of his desk and sat down in surrender, looking at Anthony as if she needed something from him.

Anthony felt his blood pressure rise and a mild exuding of sweat begin to accumulate on the backs of his arms and legs. Actually, he felt dizzy, like he had suddenly been subject to much more oxygen than he could currently breathe. A strange mixture of attraction and apprehension began to build in his body, like the welling up of groundwater, until it spilled over into his major arteries and coursed through his entire body like a surging river. However, he played it off coolly, and said to her in a voice through which Angelina could detect the minutest quiver of nervousness, "Don't you ever get tired of doing this? I mean, it's just so time consuming, you know?"

Angelina relaxed into the chair like a cat, wearing a black dress that laid upon her body like an extension of her own skin. Leaning back into the chair diagonally, she stretched out so that Anthony could see the shape of her entire body like a new alluring landscape that called out to him subliminally, beneath the guise of professionalism and work. "It definitely is," she replied casually. "That's why I really don't want to do loans anymore. I'd rather just stick to buying and selling." Her hands played upon the chair as if searching for something to touch, or as if they were waiting for something else, something more fulfilling, to happen.

"So why don't you?" Anthony answered, noticing her sinuous movements. He could detect her perfume as though it were mixed with the scent of her own sweat, mingled with whatever hidden desire had brought her to see him.

"Because!" Angelina replied coquettishly, uncrossing then crossing her legs again, as if to give Anthony a brief and tantalizing glimpse into the future. "I don't have anyone I trust to give the loans to, that's why," she said. Speaking almost teasingly, hoping she might entice him further, she said, "I need someone who will guarantee that every loan I give them will close, no matter what!" She looked at him with her large brown eyes helplessly, pleading him to assure her that everything would be okay.

"I could do that for you!" Anthony leapt at the opportunity to prove himself to Angelina, hoping to forge a more intimate connection with her.

"I'm sure you can," she smiled with gratification. "Well, let me think about it, okay?" She was playing with him like a cat plays with a mouse that it has in its clutches. She had come to him, stealthily seduced and baited him, now she'd keep him waiting for a little while just to establish her sense of control. Angelina was not unaware of her astonishing looks, or her affect upon men. And just as Anthony reveled in his own feelings of power at being able to engineer the earnings of his clients so that he could clean up on fat percentages of their loans, so Angelina reveled in her own ability to manipulate men, to make them crawl at her feet and literally adore her.

"That's fair," Anthony replied, taking note of how her entire mood had shifted from beseeching to beseeched as soon as he offered to help her.

Changing the subject so as to camouflage her strivings, Angelina asked, "So, are you excited about the Vegas contest for this month?"

"What contest?" Anthony replied, feeling his blood pressure beginning to stabilize at a higher idle. "I didn't hear anything about that."

"Oh, they talked about it at the meeting today. Weren't you there?" she asked, playing it off as though she weren't thoroughly aware of his comings and goings at work.

"Yeah I was, but I had to take off early 'cause one of my clients called." Anthony looked at her and wondered what was really going through her mind, beneath all the erroneous small talk.

"Well, I guess I can fill you in," she replied, as if it were a chore she delighted in. "It's the same as always, the top ten get to go. The only difference is that this time we can't bring anyone else with us." She looked intently into his eyes like a ray of sunlight on a dark day that suddenly pierced through the cloudbank, illuminating everything with an otherworldly glow, but only for a brief moment until it was once again swallowed up by the gloom.

At this point, Anthony felt as though he'd been drugged. He could feel some deep fissure crack and groan inside him. And he didn't know how to keep from falling in. "So," he managed to speak, dryly. "Are you sad you can't bring your man?" It wasn't the wisest thing to say in the moment, but was, for some reason, all he could manage to think of, other than the obvious.

"A little," Angelina replied, looking down at her dress and rubbing a portion of it like it was stained in order to distract her from things she didn't want to think about. "But," she continued optimistically, "I'm sure he will keep himself busy like always." Angelina felt the heat of her attraction for Anthony rise inside her like two sticks rubbing together until they sparked a fire which took hold of her and grew into a conflagration, quickly consuming the mere candle of devotion she felt for her boyfriend. As one world collided with another, and the unseen force of Eros gently rotated like a sphere on its axis, she added, more out of self-interest than mutual respect, "Is your wife going to let you go?"

"Yeah," Anthony laughed, feeling relieved that she had asked the same ridiculous, though no less important question, as he. "Why wouldn't she?"

"Oh!" Angelina exclaimed, somewhat surprised that Anthony would be so bold as to follow her lead. "Okay then, you better land some loans if you wanna have the time of your life."

"The time of my life, huh? How do you figure that?" he tested her frivolity with his own impish torment.

"Because, I'll be there. That's why!" With these words, she mocked every ounce of decency inside him. Not overtly, or even intentionally, of course. But through the razor-sharp knife that was coming dangerously close to ravaging his commitment to his wife.

"We'll see about that," Anthony replied ambiguously, although with a sheepish grin.

"You will!" Angelina promised him. A promise which he had not asked of her, but a promise nonetheless. She stood lithely from the chair as the purpose of her visit had now come to a completion, and her rumpled body elongated. "Well," she said as she turned towards the door. "I'll leave you alone so you can finish your art project." Anthony would have felt a bit embarrassed at this comment, but her intonation implied complicity, not adversity or derision. "Do you have a lot to do?" she added.

"Yeah, I do," Anthony replied, feeling muddled by strange emotions that were both exalting and disturbing.

"Well then, I'll leave you alone so you can finish up," Angelina said. Her long, sleek legs carried her to the doorway, where she looked back and added expectantly, "I'll see you around."

"Okay, Angelina," Anthony said, vexed with both longing and resignation from behind his table where he sat. "Have a good night."

Angelina passed through the doorway to the other side, and closed the door behind her. Anthony looked down at his messy desk and sighed deeply. He wondered what the hell was happening. Up until this point, he had been a happily married man. In truth, he was still happy with his wife and had no complaints about their marriage. Things were progressing smoothly between them, and they both loved each other deeply. Until Angelina had come along like some transcendent creature from the depths of his imagination, bewildering him with her beauty. She was the bombshell that was exploding his sense of stability to pieces. If he was a stronger or a wiser man, or even a more experienced man, perhaps he would have turned the other way and avoided her advances. But he was weak. He was young, and he was hungry. He was also emotionally impetuous and extremely materially ambitious, and so was she.

In the same way that Anthony had made justifications to himself about deceiving his clients so that he could profit from their loan refinancing, he also justified the possibility of having an affair with the most bodacious babe at work while remaining a married man. What the two justifications had in common were that Anthony had felt deprived of certain things his entire existence. He had grown up poor and felt he deserved the finer things in life. Although he'd always done pretty well with the ladies, he'd never fucked someone as gorgeous or sophisticated as Angelina. He reasoned to himself that perhaps her interest in him was a result of the excellent work he had provided the company, such that he'd earned it. If so, he could consider anything that transpired between them as one of the more pleasurable benefits of the job. In this way, Anthony resolved the moral dilemma he might face should things develop with Angelina. Although he had no immediate plans of action, he knew that a man had to be prepared, even if only in his mind.

Taking a deep breath, through which he attempted to release the stress and excitement of all that had just occurred, Anthony returned his attention to work. He was happy to continue alone because he had a lot of magic sticking to do that night. First off, he had to qualify a client for a new loan by changing her fico score from 580 to 780, which was an enormous leap. Then, he had to adjust a slew of late payments on the client's credit report. The new lender he'd found hadn't even pulled the customer's credit report, they just referenced Anthony's copy. It was amazing, like being able to change your grades to straight A's while no one ever knew you had flunked the class.

Before moving on to the next client, Anthony retrieved his little baggy of cocaine and poured a couple lines out on a cleared area of his desk. After doing those, he felt a bit more relaxed and freshly inspired to tackle the rest of the magic sticking. He still had to alter some tax returns from an income amount that would make most people weep to one that would incite upper middle class employees to work on a crab fishing boat off the coast of Alaska. It was a difficult task, but because the lenders only verified from the IRS very rarely, it was worth the risk. And in the back of Anthony's mind, looming over him like the towering shadow of a mere human who stood in front of a light projector, was the mirage, the illusion, the unbelievable fantasy of Angelina, who had promised him the time of his life in Vegas. So he labored on.

~ TWENTY-TWO ~

ANTHONY WORKED AS HARD as usual the remainder of the month, or so he told himself. But if you were a little green man living inside Anthony's head you could see the synapses in his brain firing at record speed—so fast, in fact, that sparks occasionally shot through the top of his head. It's true, Anthony was literally on fire and had to be sprayed down a few times with a fire extinguisher by his co-workers. He worked so hard that he sold more loans that month than anyone else, including his friend Robert who had long since recovered from his slump, and even Al. All the while, his insides worked up like the chain on a dirt bike going a hundred miles an hour, grinding with the pressure, anticipation, and unspeakable apprehension of Vegas. It's said that a man will do just about anything for money and sex. And the prospect of a rendezvous with Angelina had motivated him to achieve a higher level of success at work than anyone previously thought was possible.

Having attained the #1 sales slot at work, Anthony was impelled to share his success with Kelly. Although he was caught up in an incredible infatuation with Angelina, he still loved, admired and respected his wife. So that night he took her to one of the finest upscale restaurants in all of Irvine, one that specialized in her favorite French cuisine. As they settled into their booth at the restaurant his wife asked him, "So, are you going to tell me what we're celebrating?" She looked very pretty that evening, dressed in a deep blue gown almost the color of royal Indian ink.

"Yes I am," Anthony replied, feeling both proud and confident. "I landed more loans than anyone else and finished number one in the company this month." Kelly's eyes widened and her face brightened, as Anthony added, "And I get to go to Vegas, too."

"That's great honey," she replied. "I'm so happy for you. I know you worked really hard." Kelly admired Anthony for stepping up to the plate and devoting himself so tirelessly to his work. It gave her a feeling of reassurance and security that her man was able to exert such a powerful influence at work and bring home such hefty paychecks. Although she enjoyed the work that she did, knowing that Anthony could provide for her had also opened up the option of having kids and raising a family. She had even noticed a change in her father's demeanor towards Anthony, one which might eventually elicit his encouragement towards such a shift in their lifestyle.

"Thank you baby" Anthony replied. He could feel the love and admiration Kelly had for him as it exuded from her eyes and across the table into his. "Do you wanna know how much I made?" Anthony asked her.

"Sure, tell me!" Kelly answered excitedly.

"Ninety-eight thousand dollars." Anthony mouthed the word "thousand" slowly and with great inflection in his voice.

"What?" Kelly spoke, nearly coughing on her champagne. "Are you serious? I don't even make that in a year, honey. I'm really jealous now!" She was only teasing Anthony, but in a small, remote place inside her she felt a bit of a sting from the fact that he had been able to become so incredibly successful in such a short amount of time. Although she valued her job, she knew she had no chance of approaching the kind of money Anthony was making. Luckily, Kelly was not a competitive woman, neither with finances or with her husband, so the sting was very slight. However, she noticed its presence, alongside her overt amazement and happiness for Anthony.

After waiting for Kelly to recover from the obvious shock at hearing of his riveting paycheck, which would put him on par for making a million in a year, he decided to give her the gift he had bought her. "Don't be jealous, baby," he consoled her. "Here, this is for you." He handed her a rectangular shaped, velvet covered box. Kelly was further surprised at this, then overwhelmingly delighted as she opened the velvet box to discover its contents: a radiant diamond necklace, inlaid with blue sapphire. She gasped as she removed the necklace from the box and held it in her hands. "I know blue is your favorite color, honey. It even matches your dress."

"Oh my god! It's so beautiful, baby," Kelly exclaimed. "Thank you, sweetheart."

"No honey, you're beautiful." Anthony got up and walked around behind her to help clasp on the necklace. In that moment, Kelly felt like a superstar, or a princess, or a little girl riding a unicorn. She'd never worn such a spectacular and lustrous piece of jewelry. It made her feel rich on the inside.

While Anthony and Kelly enjoyed a romantic evening at an exquisite restaurant, meanwhile across town, Ethan, Al, Lamar, and Snowman were whoopin' it up at a ritzy bar. Actually, they were sniffin' it up, cocaine that is. Snowman was crouched in the handicap bathroom stall, intently focused on trying to do some blow by dipping his car key into the little baggy and lifting it to his nose without spilling any. Thus engaged, he was abruptly disturbed by someone banging at the bathroom stall door. Feeling an odd mixture of irritation and panic, he yelled out, "Hey! I'm using the fuckin' bathroom asshole!" But then he heard a group of guys laughing, so he quickly put his baggy away and opened up the door, whereupon he saw Ethan and the guys standing there laughing and waiting for him.

"Man!" Ethan blurted out unabashedly. "You're a fuckin' crack-head, you know that!"

Snowman looked at him perplexed, not yet amped up enough to fight, but too high already to really give a shit. He looked at the whole group and said, "You guys want some or not?"

"Of course we do asshole," Al quickly replied. "Why the fuck else would we come and track you down in the shitter!"

The guys followed Snowman back into the handicap stall and huddled around the little baggy. After taking another hit, Snowman passed the bag around and each guy snorted up what they could, using whatever method they devised on the spot. Ethan simply mimicked Snowman, and got out his own keys. Al, the most sophisticated of the four, actually had grown one pinky nail to a length which was tailored to do the job. And Lamar, also in fine fashion, strangely enough had a little spoon he wore at the end of a long silver chain necklace. It must have been new, because all the guys thought it was outrageous when they saw him pull it out of his shirt.

"Shit." Al sometimes started his sentences with this when he was stoned, stretching out his enunciation of the word as if to appreciate it's meaning to the fullest. "Did you guys see the new girl that works for escrow?"

"Hell yeah nigga," Ethan carried on the vibe. "She was fine as fuck!" He watched as Lamar snorted up a few scoops from his tiny little silver spoon and added, "She had big time ass and tits. I wanted to just grab those titties and motor boat her all day long." Ethan lowered his ass and gesticulated screwing her right there in the middle of the circle of guys in the bathroom.

"But the question is," Snowman interrupted Ethan's antics. "Would you lick her ass after she ran ten miles?"

Ethan looked up for a second as if he had to think about it. Licking his upper lip he could taste small remnants of the coke he'd just snorted. "Yeah, definitely!" he declared. "And after I did that, I'd plow her ass like John Doe!"

The guys were all high as hell, laughing and talking about how they'd sexually harangue the new hottie at work. Then, as Snowman was putting away his baggy, they were interrupted by a commanding voice outside the stall. Some impatient idiot had yelled, "Hey, you faggots done in there? I gotta take a shit!" This was too bad for him. He didn't know he'd just harassed a group of guys fired up on dope and ready to kick his ass. Before the guy knew it, Lamar came storming through the stall door and knocked him to the ground. Both Al and Ethan took it from there, pounding the shit out of his face, nearly knocking the guy unconscious. Snowman just stood there watching with a crooked expression of amusement on his face because he didn't really like to fight. Besides, he was the keeper of the baggy, and no good would come from spilling cocaine all over the guy after they'd beat him up.

After this, the guys took off from the bar, heading to another location, all four of them hoping they'd run into the new hottie from work.

~ TWENTY-THREE ~

THE BIG WEEKEND TRIP to Vegas was approaching. The month's winners had been selected, and Anthony and all of Ethan's crew were among them. Only two women had made the cut that month, one of whom was Angelina. She had kept a safe distance from Anthony over the past two weeks, since her little after hours visit to him which had sparked a carnal inferno in his solar plexus. Even so, they were both intensely aware of one another, as if an invisible radar system had formed inside their organs alerting each to the other's presence. The occasional eye contact and passing comments they made at the office only reminded both of them of the enormous underlying energy they were holding in check. Fortunately, no one else had picked up on any of this, so it hadn't bled into the social realm of gossip.

A few days later, the top eight loan officers of Fairtex Mortgage Company, accompanied by Lister and Thomas Blake, walked through the glamorous casino in Vegas on their way to the penthouse hotel that awaited them. (Both Angelina and Loretta, the other winning female loan officer, had opted to take a later flight together in order to finish up some business.) Looking like a group that had just walked out of GQ Magazine, the men were all dressed in their finest, most expensive duds, and strutted along like peacocks showing off their flair. They were young and cocky and ready for action, as they attracted attention from desirous women and other envious men. They had spent the previous four weeks working their asses off and had made a boat load of cash; now they were being rewarded for it. The company had flown them to Vegas, and they were ready to unload. Come what may, they had done their work and were ready for a wild weekend.

As everyone filed into the hotel, the extravagance of the place began to hit them. The bottom floor featured botanical gardens and a pristine courtyard with a gorgeous pool and a hot tub. There were saunas and massage parlors as well, and incredible paintings lined the walls of the lobby. Fairtex had rented the entire top floor of the hotel, so they had a virtual millionaire's campground in which to party for the entire weekend. As they exited the elevator on the top floor, they passed through the executive lounge area which featured an old style cedar wood pool table and a bar stocked with just about every kind of whiskey, scotch, and vodka you could imagine. The view of the city was impeccable, it was brilliant and stunning as they all gazed out into the hot landscape from which they had just come. The suites themselves were fabulous too, featuring marble foyers and bathrooms with enclosed glass steam showers, huge flat screen TVs with built-in sound systems and a million internet music options. And, of course, lush California King beds.

"Oh shit," Ethan virtually yelped. "This is sick!"

"Damn," Anthony added, having never been in such luxurious surroundings, "I can't believe this shit!"

"It's alright!" Al chimed in pompously. "But I've been in better suites." He casually tested the bed with his hand and shrugged as if it passed the test.

"Alright big baller, we know you have!" Lamar countered. "But don't shit on our parade, man. I mean, this place is fuckin' off the hook!"

"Fuck yeah," Ethan agreed. "This is the nicest room I've ever seen."

"And it's gonna be one crazy weekend! That's for damn sure," Lamar said.

Thomas Blake had come up to the top floor penthouse suite with the loan officers, although he was staying in another undisclosed suite, private from their floor. He enjoyed seeing the delight on their faces and hearing the enchantment in their voices as they all milled around the suite. "So, you guys like the place?" he announced to everyone in the group.

A collective praise for the lodgings issued from the group, and Anthony's voice rose above them all, exclaiming "Yes sir! Thank you very much. It's incredible!"

"Well, you guys definitely deserve it," Blake replied happily. "Keep up the good work and there's plenty more of this to come."

"Thank you, sir," said Ethan. He usually wasn't much for formalities, but in the case of Thomas Blake, Ethan recognized the man who was responsible for enabling him to become more rich than he ever imagined he could. And in some not yet strangled portion of Ethan's dried out heart, he really appreciated Blake.

"Okay," Blake clapped his hands together as if he had just called the deciding play in a college football huddle. "Now all of you get ready. The limo will pick us up in one hour!" He smiled nearly lasciviously, but with an enduring sense of self-integrity, and added, "We have bottle service waiting for us gentlemen! I'll see you all downstairs in an hour." There was a general brouhaha amongst the loan officers, an upheaval of all their hopes and expectations about the weekend. Then, as they had all been given key cards with room numbers, everyone gradually dispersed to their own private suites.

On the way to theirs, Anthony said to Ethan, "Where's Angelina?"

"Don't worry bro, she'll come," he said, giving Anthony a little shove and looking at him mischievously as they walked down the hallway. "She and Loretta had to take a later flight."

"Oh shit, it's not like I care!" Anthony protested. "I was just wondering where she was, that's all!"

"Yeah, right." Ethan looked at Anthony like he was full of shit as he located and opened the door to his own room, and told him he'd see him soon down in the lobby.

Later that night, the entire group went to an upscale Vegas nightclub. Although there was a line of people waiting outside to get in, the company had procured VIP passes for them, so they moved to the front of the line and walked in without waiting. The club was boomin' on the inside. Throngs of people dressed to the hilt with glitter and glam and perfumed copiously moved about the floor drinking and dancing. The walls were chiseled in mesmerizing geometrical shapes, with brilliant lights pulsating upon them. Chunks of crystalline beads hung in long strands from the ceiling in places, like new wave chandeliers. The bar was translucent with an aqua marine blue light shining through it, and there were intriguing art designs on the floor lit up with embedded lights inside them. The place was dazzling as the group made their way to the VIP section of the club.

Angelina was waiting for them there, looking shockingly sexy. Two beautiful hostesses worked the private bar, but neither one could compare to the sublime elegance of Angelina. As the group filed in, she exclaimed to them all, "Hi boys! What took you so long?"

"Anthony took forever to put his make up on," Snowman said tongue-in-cheek, and a few of the guys chuckled. "Sorry 'bout that sugar."

"Oh did he?" Angelina egged him on.

Even Anthony thought it was funny, but being an alpha he had to defend himself and said, "Don't listen to these jerk-offs." Then he added, "Glad you could make it Angelina. How was your private flight?"

She smiled flirtatiously at Anthony and said it was fine. However, she maintained eye contact a bit too long and without notice Anthony felt something hot and sharp suddenly rupture inside him, like a pipe that had unexpectedly busted, sending hot spurts of water through his heart and his groin. She could feel it too. And her eyes suggested an impending deluge. Meanwhile, the hostesses handed out tequila shots to everyone, and Thomas Blake christened the party saying, "Everyone, let's do a toast before we all split up. This is to all your hard work! Cheers!"

A general uproar of joyful pandemonium resounded from the group as everyone downed their first shot, instigating the official start of the night's mayhem. With his first drink, Anthony broke off the unbearable torment of eye contact with Angelina, and he and Ethan wandered around the club to check it out. Meanwhile, Al and Snowman worked a small gaggle of girls on the dance floor and Lamar struck out on his own, eventually smooth-talking a hot Persian doll at the bar.

After downing a few more drinks, Ethan and Anthony ended up in the bathroom to snort some coke. It was good shit and gave them both the lift they needed to meet the high velocity of Vegas. Ethan had seen a few girls he liked, but had no luck with any of them yet. The cocaine sometimes gave him the extra push he needed to get outside of his own anxious skin and make something happen. At least that's what he was hoping for this night. As they left the bathroom and walked back towards the VIP section, Anthony saw Angelina on the dance floor. She was looking right at him like a rifle scoped in on its target. As Anthony stopped, letting his friend walk on, she motioned to him with her finger to come join her.

~ TWENTY-FOUR ~

ANGELINA SLID THE CARD through the sensor on the door to her own private suite at the hotel and walked in with Anthony trailing right behind her. They were both lit up with drink, but not too drunk to realize they should avoid being seen making out at the nightclub by the other loan officers. Once inside her room, Anthony closed the door and Angelina turned around directly, igniting his lips with a fiery kiss. Anthony pushed away from the wall and turned her so that he was pressing Angelina against an adjoining wall. They made out hard for a few minutes, both of them furiously fondling and undressing one another. Anthony slipped off her dress, and began kissing her neck and shoulders. As he moved around to her breasts, he got her bra off and set to kissing and sucking her tits. He moved down to her belly, kissing and caressing her. Then suddenly, like a geyser rising out of the ground, he lifted her up and carried her to the bed where he slammed her down and leapt on top of her, and they fucked like wild animals in heat.

After an hour or so, although it seemed like a small slice of eternity to them, Anthony and Angelina rested on the bed in stillness and refrain. "So, do you wanna know what I was thinking?" Angelina asked Anthony in the calm that followed the storm.

"What's that?" Anthony replied, laying beside her.

"I decided I wanna give you all my loans from now on," she said, as she sat propped up on one elbow looking down at him and smiled.

"Really?" Anthony replied, not quite wanting the weightless moment of surrender in which he was suspended to end, but also piqued by the proposition that Angelina would want to conspire so closely with him at work. "Are you sure?" he added.

"Yeah, I am," she said softly, gently brushing the side of his face affectionately. "I trust you more than anyone else."

Anthony was impelled by her trust in him and replied, "I won't let you down, okay?"

"I had a feeling you'd say that," she giggled.

After a few moments of silence in which Anthony collected his thoughts, he said, "Can I ask you something?

"Sure."

"Why are you with that asshole?"

"I don't know," she replied, looking down and searching for the right thing to say. "I guess he makes me happy."

"Why, because he buys you anything you want?" Anthony wanted to know how such an arrogant idiot could attract a woman as beautiful and sophisticated and extravagant as Angelina.

"No, not really," she laughed. "But that sure helps." Turning the question around on him, she asked, "So why are you with Kelly?"

Anthony felt a heaviness in his body. Perhaps it came from his heart, but he felt it all throughout him. "Because I love her," he answered reluctantly.

"Well, I don't know about that," Angelina object-ed. Although she sounded sure of herself, at bottom she was really nervous. She knew Anthony's marriage ran much deeper than her own passing fling with her current boyfriend, but she didn't want to admit it. "Maybe in the beginning you were in love with her, but when I see you with her now I don't get the feeling that you are any-more." She paused before adding, "Do you wanna know what type of girl you need in your life?"

"Umm. Your type?" Anthony replied humorously.

"The type of woman that has the same kinds of ambitions that you have in life," she said with an air of self-assuredness.

"I see," Anthony replied, feeling amused.

"And to answer your question," Angelina contin-ued. "A woman like me would probably be perfect for a guy like you." She kissed him, and they both turned to-wards one another, once again becoming submerged in each other's bodies.

~ TWENTY-FIVE ~

ANTHONY SAT AT HIS DESK at Fairtex Mortgage on a Wednesday morning later the next month. He was exhausted. Now that Angelina was giving him seven to ten loans a week he was so busy that he had to clock in at six a.m. in the morning and didn't go home until ten at night. He also stopped cold calling because he was sending out mailers instead. In the letters, each homeowner had his or her current mortgage company's name; so when the homeowner called Anthony, he or she already thought that Anthony was their lender, and it made everything that much easier. He was getting so many calls that he had to hire two college girls just to help keep up with the new clients. He was submitting two to three loans every day and didn't have a month where he made less then hundred and forty thousand dollars a month.

The phone rang, and he picked up, "This is Anthony, how can I help you?"

On the other end of the line, a familiar client had called him. Ms. Gonzalez was a single mom in her forties and getting ready to sign loan documents. "Yes, hello. This is Maria Gonzalez."

Anthony was immediately concerned because Ms. Gonzalez was supposed to be signing her loan with the notary he had sent to her house, and clients rarely called him unless there was some serious problem. "Hi Maria, is everything going okay at your signing?" Anthony inquired.

"No Anthony, it's not. I've decided I don't want to sign on this loan."

"What do you mean Ms. Gonzalez?" Anthony replied. "Why don't you want to sign?"

"Well," she was overweight and a little out of breath, just trying to explain herself. "I talked to another broker, and he said he can get me five point seven five percent on this loan."

"Okay ma'am," Anthony said, knowing exactly where this phone call was going. "And we're offering you a five point eight seven five percent, right?"

"Yes, that's right Anthony."

"Well, we definitely want to keep your business with us, considering we are your current lender. Give me a minute to contact the lock desk and see what I can do for you, okay Maria?"

"Okay, sure." Ms. Gonzalez had nowhere to go, and she was certainly willing to wait and see if she could get a better rate on the loan.

"Okay then. I'm gonna put you on hold, but I'll be right back." Although he knew he could reel her back in, just like a fish on a hook, Anthony wasn't really in the mood for it today. So he opened a desk drawer and pulled out his little baggy of blow. He quickly poured out a couple of lines and sorted them. *The fuckin' bitch*, Anthony thought to himself, *trying to pull that shit on me at the last second.* He shook his head getting ready to pick up on the line again when he heard a knock at his office door.

"Come in!" Anthony barked. The door quickly opened and in walked Shannon, one of Anthony's young, attractive college assistants.

"Oh, sorry. Were you busy?"

"No … well actually yes," Anthony said in confusion as he stuffed his baggy back into the drawer and brushed away the evidence. "I'm on the phone with a client, what's up?"

"I just wanted to let you know I have the applications ready from this morning!" Shannon proclaimed excitedly. She took a lot of pride in being helpful to such an important man as Anthony Cousto. Noticing his ragged demeanor, she commented, "Wow, you don't look so good, boss." She closed the door and walked briskly over to Anthony and stood behind him. Placing her hands on his shoulder she asked, "Do you need a massage?"

"Sure Shannon. That would be great," he replied, as he picked up the phone to continue his call.

"Maria! Sorry about putting you on hold."

"Oh, that's no problem Anthony," she reassured him.

"So, I spoke with the lock desk and they said they're willing to lower your rate to five point five percent." As Anthony spoke, Shannon massaged him, gradually lowering her hands, moving down Anthony's back until she came to his waist line. She slowly circled her hands around to the front of his body and grabbed his package full on, massaging his cock through his pants. She then moved around to the front of him and got down on her knees and unbuttoned his pants, continuing to rub his cock. Then she proceeded to give him a first class blowjob.

Anthony was exquisitely shocked by this, as he managed to continue his phone conversation with Ms. Gonzalez; however, his voice broke a few times. "Umm! But since your lock expires in 4 days, you're going to have to sign all the documents today at five point eight seven five percent. Tomorrow, I'll send the amended documents for you to sign. Will that work for you Maria?"

"Yes," Ms. Gonzalez answered slowly. "That's fine, I trust you Anthony."

"Okay, great!" Anthony spoke as if it was a matter of immediate importance, but really he was just struggling to keep up with the surge of pleasure Shannon was providing him. "Can I please talk to the notary really quick?"

Ms. Gonzalez gave the phone to the notary who was there to help her process the loan.

"Hi, this is Brenda."

"Hey Brenda, Anthony here. So, just sign the loan and agree with everything she says, okay?"

"Sure, no problem! Thank you Anthony," she said, eager to complete the loan.

After that, Anthony simply hung up the phone and focused his full attention on the unsolicited luxurious side-service he was now receiving underneath his desk. He leaned back in his chair and fully enjoyed another of the fringe benefits that came with being a big shot.

Regarding the loan, however, Anthony had absolutely no plans to lower the lady's rate. In fact, the next day he would come up with some excuse of how the documents weren't ready, and before she even knew it the loan would get funded. By the time she realized she wasn't getting what Anthony had promised it would be too late for her to do anything. But that's how it worked at Fairtex Mortgage: another day, another thousand dollars sucked from the hearts of each client's trusted bank account. It was lecherous. They weren't really refinancing anyone's loans. What they were really doing was finding excuses to attach themselves like leeches to the fruits of other peoples labors, and to suck out as much as they could. *But, so what?* Anthony thought to himself. *That's the way of the world: Capitalism at its finest!*

~ TWENTY-SEVEN ~

WHAT GOES UP must come down. And so, Anthony's impetuous joyride was about to come to an unexpected crossroads. Arriving home one day to his new mansion, he pulled into the driveway and got out of his bright red Ferrari. Walking to the house he noticed the front door was eerily wide open. As he entered the house, he heard an occasional thumping sound, as if something were flopping down on the floor in the living room. As he turned the corner, he saw a haphazard pile of clothing on the fine cherry wood floor, along with random articles of clothing trailing down the banner and the steps. The clothes were, in fact, his own.

His curiosity now thoroughly provoked, he continued on to the stairs and began to climb them, attempting not to slip on his own dirty skivvies. About midway up, he received a face-full of laundry as Kelly had briefly appeared at the top of the stairs and thrown them down at him. He shrugged off the clothing and continued up the stairs. When he had arrived at the top of the stairs, Kelly had returned with another armload of his clothing and was prepared to throw them at him when he stopped her by wrapping his arms around her.

"Hey," he said. "What are you doing, honey? What the fuck is going on?"

At this, she began to sob and struggled to free herself from his hold, screaming, "I hate you Anthony! I hate you!" Choking on her own tears, she continued, "How could you do this to me?"

"What are you talking about," he replied, not yet fully aware of the severity of the situation. "What did I do?"

This kind of denial from her husband completely infuriated her and she slapped him hard across the face before turning away. She went to the nightstand by their bed and retrieved a yellow envelope. Opening it as she walked back towards him, she flashed a photograph of Anthony and Angelina on one of their San Francisco getaways, and then threw it at him. "What did you do?!?" she yelled, mocking him. "What the fuck is this Anthony!?! Huh?" Anthony stood there motionless, not knowing what to do or say. Then she yelled at him more loudly and with greater vehemence, "How long have you been fucking her, you piece of shit?!?" Her face shook with rage and she turned beet red as she threw the whole envelope of photos at him. As he stood there paralyzed in silence she cried out, "Well, are you going to tell me!?!"

"You had someone follow me?" Anthony stammered.

"Yeah, I did! I knew you didn't have to work out of town all the time, you fuckin' liar! Why did you do this to me?"

Anthony approached her again, just to hold her because he could think of nothing to say. But she was terribly angry, so angry that she slapped him full on the face again, leaving a small welt by his eye.

"I'm sorry Kelly," Anthony said regretfully and in pain. "It just happened!" He mumbled indiscernible words, not knowing what to say and trying to get a hold of himself, trying to determine what to do. He could think of nothing, so he said the only thing that he knew was true. "But I love you so much!"

"What do you mean it just happened?? How could you do that to me?" She was sobbing, but also still fiercely infuriated. "I've always been there for you, even when you didn't have shit, you fucking asshole!" Kelly was yelling hysterically, beyond all self-control and out of her mind with agony. "And this is how you show your love to me?!? By fucking some whore at work?!?" She picked up another bunch of his belongings off a chest of drawers and threw them at him yelling, "Fuck you, Anthony!"

Anthony was beside himself with guilt and angst. He was totally confused, stupefied and frozen with anxiety. He'd been found out, and now it was time to pay the piper. Hoping she would somehow forgive him, at least for one brief moment, he approached her again as if to hold her. But she was not ready for that, maybe she never would be. In that moment, she was truly beyond comprehension with disgust and rage, so she turned him away, slapping him a third time on the same side of his face that was already red and swollen with pain.

Looking at him as if he was a stranger, as if he was an intruder in her home, she shouted, "You know what, Anthony, I want you to leave. Get out! Get out right now and don't come back! Leave me alone! Please! Go! Leave!!!" Her voice shrieked as her commands intermingled with sobs of sadness.

At this, she abruptly left him and went to the bathroom to cry alone. Anthony heard the door lock followed by her heavy sobs within. Filled with sadness and remorse, Anthony turned away from their bed, descended the madness of the steps and left the house, closing the front door behind him, not knowing when he would return.

~ TWENTY-EIGHT ~

Anthony was distraught. He didn't know where
to go, so he drove to Angelina's place. He knocked on the
front door a few times before she answered. His face was
bruised and she could see dried tear stains under his eyes.

"What's wrong baby?" she asked, very concerned
and stepping out of the doorway to be nearer to him.

Looking almost like an old and deteriorated statue
of himself, Anthony replied, "Kelly found us out."

"Shit, are you serious?" she exclaimed. Then she
embraced him.

"Yeah, she had someone follow us while we were
in San Francisco. I'm not sure which time, but she had pic-
tures." Anthony had been sad, but he was nearly snarling
as he said this. He was offended that someone had actually tracked them down, observed and photographed them
without their knowing a damn thing. He wondered how
long he'd been trailed and to what extent.

"She did?" Angelina was very surprised too. "Oh
my god! I'm so sorry." Ever so gently she touched the side
of Anthony's face and he winced. "Jesus, she really hit you
hard. What are you gonna do?"

"I don't know," Anthony replied, thinking intently, or at least trying to. He was in a state of shock. His

whole life and marriage with Kelly was dissolving right before his eyes in one short afternoon, and he just couldn't believe it. "Do you think I should go back?" he muttered absentmindedly, not realizing that would be just about the stupidest thing he could do at the time.

"No, don't do that," Angelina wisely replied. "It will just make things worse. I think she needs some time alone. Why don't you just stay here tonight and see what happens tomorrow. Okay, baby?" She put her arms around his neck and kissed him on the lips. Then she pulled back a little and looked into his eyes. "Look at me!" she said. "I'm here for you okay? So try not to worry so much about it. Everything will be fine, I promise. We'll, get through this together." She hugged him, and kissed him again, then took him by the hand and led him into the safe harbor of her condo and closed the door behind them.

~ TWENTY-NINE ~

THE NEXT DAY, Anthony called his dad and asked if he could meet him at a local pub. He told him briefly about the situation with Kelly over the phone, but said he'd rather meet in person to discuss it at length. At the bar, Anthony sat in a booth waiting for his father. He'd gotten there early and ordered a pitcher of MGD with two glasses. He was tired and worried and confused. But the beer was refreshing, and the sight of his dad walking through the door consoled him a bit. "How are you dad?" he said, standing to hug him. As he sat back down in the booth, he added, "Damn, I really got myself into a mess this time, huh?"

"Yes, you did son," his father answered with a mild scowl. Situating himself on the black booth cushion seat he added, "So, who's this girl Angelina, eh?"

Anthony felt embarrassed and admitted, "She's a woman I work with."

"I see," his father said. After reflecting a moment, he asked, "Do you love her?"

This was a question Anthony had also asked himself, and one which he wasn't sure he could answer. "I don't know," he replied, taking another swig of beer. "I mean, we have a lot of fun together and we both have a lot of the same goals."

"Hmmm," his father replied, as Anthony poured him a fresh glass of chilled beer. "What kind of goals would those be?"

"I don't know dad," Anthony said, feeling a bit frustrated and pressured. At that moment, he was at his wit's end and just wanted to be understood. "To be successful and make money, I guess."

"I see," his dad replied, taking his first sip of beer. "Well son, I've told you before and I'll tell you again, money isn't everything."

"Maybe not to you dad, but it's damn important to me!" Anthony quipped.

"How's that?" his dad questioned him.

"Come on dad," Anthony bargained, feeling put on the spot. "I'm not doing this right now."

"Why not?" his dad implored, adjusting his glasses, then rapping his knuckles on the table. "C'mon son, tell me why money means so much to you?"

"Because with enough money I can have whatever I want!" Anthony exclaimed. "Is that what you wanna hear?"

His father looked down at the table disappointedly and shook his head in disbelief. "Material things are not all that important, son. Most of the things that money can buy you don't need anyway. Like that stupid car of yours! Why do you need a two-hundred-and-fifty-thousand-dollar car? When you get old and you can't work anymore, that's when you'll really need your money, just to live. I told you to save for your future, and what do you do? The exact opposite!" Anthony's father felt exasperated with his son. He didn't understand why he was so money-hungry, so endlessly driven to become more and more wealthy. He looked outside the bar as if searching his mind for the right thing to say to his son. "Listen to me son," he said. "There are other things that matter than money."

"Yeah, like what pop?" Anthony countered.

"Well, like love, for one. Let me ask you this," his father continued, thinking about his own marriage with Anthony's mom, "do you think this girl, Angelina, will stick around if you lose everything, all your precious belongings and all your money?"

"That's not gonna happen dad!" Anthony protested.

"Okay, fine. But what if it does?"

"Well, it's a stupid question! I will never let that happen," Anthony ranted, "so there's no reason to answer it."

"All I'm trying to say is that Kelly loves you no matter what, and she will always stick by your side. That's the type of woman you should be with Anthony. She was there for you when you had no money, remember that? You don't know if this girl will be." His father looked Anthony over and exclaimed with a regretful measure of repugnance, "I didn't raise you to be like this!"

Anthony was shocked that his dad would say such a thing, and he quickly replied, "Like what dad?"

Feeling an unusual wave of anger rise in him towards his son, Anthony's father said, "Look at yourself, all you care about is money! How much did those glasses cost you, or your highfalutin shirt, or your millionaire's watch, huh?"

At this, Anthony felt pissed off, insulted that his dad would reproach him for spending the hard earned money he'd worked to make himself. He wasn't usually rude or disrespectful with his dad, but in this moment he felt raw and hurt and angry, and he couldn't keep himself from saying exactly what he thought. "You know dad, don't be mad at me for actually doing something with my life. Unlike you!"

The last comment had been too much for Anthony's dad to take, and he stood up to leave saying, "I don't have to listen to this crap! Remember, you asked me to come here. Now I'm leaving." At this, he picked up his hat and walked out of the bar.

Anthony felt upset and frustrated. He'd already devastated his wife and didn't need to cause more turmoil with his own family. He pulled a twenty dollar bill out of his wallet and threw it down on the table. Then he picked up his jacket and hurried outside to catch up with his dad. But then his temper caught up with him too. "Where you going dad? You know I'm right!" Anthony called out to his father once he got outside. Catching up to him in the parking lot he said, "You're just jealous of me, is that it, dad?"

His father looked at him as though Anthony were crazy. "Jealous of what?" he gasped reaching to get his keys out of his pocket.

"That I'm making all this money and you never made shit!" Anthony continued to yell. "Do you want me to tell you why you never made anything dad? 'Cause you never took any risks in life. All you ever did was drive that fuckin' cab, and that's exactly why I wanna make money, so my kids don't go through the shit I did."

"If that's the way you think, then I did a horrible job of raising you Anthony. I told you before, life is not about money!"

"Bullshit! Everything has to do with money," Anthony yelled. Unable to control his anger, he continued, "Maybe if you actually did something with your life you could see that. You think I don't remember when I would wear the same clothes to school year after year, or when you and mom would argue about money all the time?

How can you stand here and tell me life isn't about money? Welcome to the real world dad! Look around! Everything revolves around money, you just never had the balls to open your eyes and see it. Maybe if you did you'd actually have something to show for your life!"

After a moment of silent shock, Anthony's dad responded, "I didn't know you felt like that about me." He felt deeply, nearly unspeakably hurt that his own son had reproached him like this. "I'm sorry I couldn't give you a better life, but I tried my best to give you everything I could. I guess it just wasn't enough for you. I'm sorry!" Getting into his cab, Anthony's dad refused to talk anymore. He pulled away from the parking lot, his tires squealing as he turned too fastly into the road.

~ THIRTY ~

ANTHONY SPENT THE NEXT FEW DAYS and nights at Angelina's place before receiving a brief email from Kelly stating that she was going to leave their home to stay with her mother for awhile. He'd had difficulty sleeping at Angelina's and felt terribly guilty about how his affair had affected Kelly. They hadn't talked since the horrible day she had confronted him at the house about his affair, and he was truly concerned and uncertain about what would happen. However, he also didn't like being away from his home with all his things and familiar surroundings for so long. Upon receiving the email from Kelly, he decided to go home, and this, at least, abated his discomfort with feeling physically dislocated and misplaced. Although he and Angelina had managed to keep things cool at work without betraying their situation to their co-workers, Anthony had been anxious to get back to the stable base of his own home, to regroup and hopefully think more clearly about everything.

Anthony also hadn't talked with his dad since their blowout, and he felt bad about laying into him so hard about his job as a taxi cab driver. Their argument weighed heavy on his mind as he drove to work that day. He wanted to apologize, but he needed to let the dust settle a bit before he called his dad again. He was planning to return to his own home after work that day, and he knew this would be a big relief for him, perhaps the first necessary step in resolving all his problems.

Arriving at work that day, Anthony was greeted by his assistant Shannon who approached him anxiously on the sales room floor saying, "Good morning boss. Ms. Gonzalez is on the phone, and she sounds really upset!"

"Alright," Anthony replied, continuing to walk towards his office. "Send her through to my desk and I'll handle it." Anthony entered the private quarters of his office. It was a rather plush scenario, with burgundy leather high-back swivel chairs, a leather-topped mahogany desk, and beautiful carpet and wallpaper. They had done a fine job of decorating the room for Anthony and he felt thoroughly appreciated by the company, especially David Konn and Thomas Blake. As he sat down on the chair behind his desk, he thought about doing some blow. He'd been developing a habit lately and, while he knew it wasn't good for him, he felt he needed something to keep him going under such incredibly unusual and stressful circumstances. Not only was work a monumental bitch, his wife had left him, and the whole façade of his marriage was beginning to crumble down. The coke at least helped to pick him up and made him feel temporarily satisfied.

As he pulled out the little white baggy and cut a line on his desk, the phone rang. He snorted up the line as the phone continued to ring, then stashed the baggy back in his desk. After wiping his face clean and forcefully sniffing the air to make sure there was no leftover cocaine powder inside his nostrils, Anthony finally picked up the phone.

"Hi, Ms. Gonzalez. How are you?" He spoke distractedly, as if it didn't much matter to him how Ms. Gonzalez was really doing.

"I'm not doing very well Anthony!" Ms. Gonzalez spoke angrily.

"Why? What's going on ma'am?" Anthony questioned, knowing fairly well that she was calling about the loan. As he asked her this question, Shannon came into the room and sat down in front of his desk to listen in on the conversation. She knew she'd also probably be dealing with Ms. Gonzalez as well, so she wanted to be kept informed about the situation. Also, this sort of wheeling and dealing was new to her, so she had a lot to learn about how things worked at Fairtex Mortgage.

"You told me to sign the documents and that the bank would lower my rate to 5.5% 30 year fixed." Ms. Gonzalez spoke rapidly in a Mexican accent that was somewhat hard for Anthony to follow, but he got the gist of what she was saying. "You also told me, Anthony, that this was not a negative amortization loan." When Ms. Gonzalez said the word "amortization," a word that would be difficult for anyone to say correctly, she pronounced it as if it were "a-mortal-ization," a faux pas which made Anthony smile in the midst of the tension he was now feeling.

"Correct," Anthony said, agreeing with her summary of their recent conversation.

"Well, I just received my mortgage statement and the rate is still 5.875%, and it's giving me 4 payment options. I also had my sister look at it, and she told me that I had a negative amortization loan, too. Anthony I trusted you! How could you do this to me?" Ms. Gonzalez had an accusatory tone in her voice. She obviously felt she had been misled and betrayed by Anthony. Anthony, on the other hand, was thinking hard of a way to weasel out of responsibility for the deceptive promises he had made to his client.

"Wait a second Ms. Gonzalez. I didn't do anything," Anthony quickly defended himself. "When I talked
to the bank, they were supposed to fix everything. So if
they dropped the ball, please don't blame me. But listen,
here's what I can do for you. I'll call the bank right now
and see what went wrong." Anthony had learned very
well the art of deflecting the blame for his faulty loan
promises onto the lenders. And it usually worked. As long
as the clients had someone to reproach for their bad loan
other than Anthony, they would usually continue to work
with him. "Just do me a favor, and fax me the mortgage
statement so I can see what you're talking about. I will let
you know this; if the bank for any reason doesn't work
with us, I'll execute a new loan for you with no charge at
all, and at the correct rate. Will that work for you Ms.
Gonzalez?"

Anthony could hear the ire in her voice decrease as
the influence of his conniving subterfuge was beginning to
take effect. "Okay Anthony," Ms. Gonzalez replied. "But
what about the prepayment penalty? If we do a new loan,
will I have to pay that?"

"No ma'am, not at all," he reassured her. "I'll take
care of that for you."

"You promise you will, Anthony?" Ms. Gonzalez
sounded more like she was pleading than demanding.
"You know this house is all I have, and I can't lose it."

"I understand. And I won't let that happen to you
Ms. Gonzalez."

"Okay. I'll fax the mortgage statement to you, and
please see what you can do." Unfortunately for her, Ms.
Gonzalez was willing to trust Anthony one more time.
Since he had originally fed her the idea of undercutting
the other lender with a lower rate, she had become reluc-
tant to believe that it just wasn't possible. Ironically, her

own insistent frugality was causing her to jeopardize her finances.

"I will ma'am, don't worry," Anthony said. Then he cut her off by adding, "Looks like I have another call coming in, so I'll get back to you next week, okay?"

"Alright, thank you Anthony. Talk to you next week."

"Sure, no problem. Take care Ms. Gonzalez." Anthony hung up the phone, and looked at Shannon as if he were expecting her to ask him a question.

"So, what do you want to do with her?" Shannon quickly queried.

"Another fuckin' loan that's what," Anthony replied sarcastically, although he was being completely serious. "Submit it today."

"What about the pre-payment penalty?" Shannon inquired.

Leaning back in his chair to relax for a brief moment, Anthony answered her very logical question by stating, "She's gonna have to pay it, so include it in her new loan amount. And make sure you charge her at least five grand for our fees; I'm not doing this shit for free." He made a gesture with his hand expressing his inherent disregard for helping Ms. Gonzalez. He had succeeded in getting her off his back for another week, and that's all that mattered to him right now.

"Whatever you say," Shannon replied, noting that Anthony had appeared to be extremely stressed out recently. She got up to leave, figuring it was better to let him recover from his bad mood alone. Anthony returned his attention to the new accounts on his desk. He'd fallen a little behind this week and needed to catch up with ensuring a bunch of new loan applications were refinanced. Throughout the day he worked mostly alone, processing loans and making a few calls. However, he was continually distracted by the thought of returning to his home that night. Knowing that Kelly wouldn't be there made a deep empty hole of sadness inside him.

Later in the day, Anthony returned home. The house was dark as he pulled into the driveway. Opening the front door, he walked to the living room and put down his briefcase. He continued on to the kitchen for a glass of water and noticed a large manila envelope addressed to him on the counter. His heart sunk inside him as he opened the envelope and found divorce documents Kelly had drawn up to serve him. Although he knew it had been possible, the immediate prospect of divorce made him feel dizzy, as though he were suspended in outer space with no reference point for reality. He felt his blood grow cold and had the sensation that his very soul was fragmenting, cracking like glacial ice or the baked earth of a desert floor, pieces falling off and dispersing into an unknown ether which he could not conceive. He felt a sudden and pro-foundly disturbing loneliness shoot through him like an arrow.

With nothing better to do than pour himself a drink, Anthony grabbed the whiskey and a highball glass, and went out to the patio. He sat down and lit a cigarette in the dark. Taking a long sip of whiskey, he felt himself falling into the abyss.

THIRTY-ONE

THE NEXT MORNING, Anthony showed up at work on time as always. Entering through the front lobby, the receptionist greeted him, "Good morning Anthony. Mr. Blake would like to see you in his office immediately."

"Okay, thank you," Anthony managed to say without revealing how tired and forlorn he really felt. Making his way across the sales room floor, Anthony went to Mr. Blake's office before even going to his own. He figured if something was up, he wanted to know about it right away. After knocking on the door, Anthony heard Mr. Blake's voice call out for him to come in. Upon opening the door, Anthony saw that Mr. Blake was not alone. In fact, his office was filled with Anthony's entire sales team; even David Konn was there.

"There he is!" Al was the first to speak out. And with this the entire room clapped while looking in admiration at Anthony.

"That's the man we've been looking for," Mr. Blake said cheerfully.

"Congratulations buddy!" David Konn added.

Anthony was completely clueless as to what everyone was talking about. But he played along and smiled just the same.

"Man," Al exclaimed. "I can't believe this guy broke my record! Look at him, he looks like he hasn't slept for weeks."

"I can believe it!" Lister belched. Then, looking at Anthony he added, "You're fuckin' killin' it bro!" and high-fived him vehemently.

"Calm down everyone," Mr. Blake said, but he was talking mainly to Lister. Then, to Anthony, he stated, "Anthony, your team, David, and I wanted to personally congratulate you on your record-breaking month." He handed Anthony a plain white envelope branded with the Fairtex Mortgage Company logo and added, "This envelope contains the single biggest check I have ever written to anyone. And you deserve it!"

"Thank you sir," Anthony replied, humbly accepting the envelope from Mr. Blake.

"Mr. Blake, are you gonna tell us what he did!" Snowman asked excitedly.

"I sure am," Blake proudly replied. "Forty loans with over four hundred thousand dollars in rev. All in one month!"

"Fuck! That's official big dog!" Snowman exclaimed. This was the first time all the guys had heard the numbers, and they were not only shocked, they were seriously impressed.

"That's my boy!" Ethan added. He could barely believe that it was possible to land so many loans and so much rev in month.

"Those are big numbers Anthony. That's really good shit, man!" Lamar said. For once in his life, at least at Fairtex Mortgage, Al was simply speechless. He and the other guys proceeded to circle around Anthony and shake his hand and pat him on the back while uttering their own personal words of congratulations.

Although Anthony enjoyed the praise, it was painfully hard for him to accept. Having recently come to the inner conviction that what he was doing at work was really wrong, was really unethical and harmful to others, he only wanted to tell his co-workers that he had made all that money by lying, cheating and deceiving his clients through severely manipulating their loan information. But how could he? He was their hero for the day, and he didn't want to piss on anyone's fireworks. So he celebrated with them and accepted the honor, all along feeling like a shell that was about to break.

~ THIRTY-TWO ~

LATER IN THE DAY, Anthony took a walk to the park near his office just to clear his head. He made it to his favorite spot towards the middle of the park and sat down on a bench in the midst of a natural tranquility. However, it was completely ironic because inside himself Anthony felt more miserable and chaotic than he ever had. Yeah, he was holding a check for $280,000 in his hands, probably the largest paycheck he would ever make in one month. But he felt like a complete fake. Not only had he lied to his clients and deceived them to make all that money, but he had also lied to his wife and deceived her until she found him out. And now it had probably cost him his marriage.

Feeling like the only person in the world who could retrieve him from sordid state was his wife, he pulled his cell phone from his pocket and dialed her number. After ringing four or five times, her voicemail came on and Anthony hung up disgruntled without leaving a message. As soon as he had shoved his cell phone back into his pants pocket, it began to ring. Thinking it was Kelly, he quickly pulled it back out, but as he looked at the screen he saw that it was his mom calling. He answered the phone and heard her crying as she said, "Anthony, your dad got in a car accident."

"What!" Anthony exclaimed with worry. "Is he okay?"

"No, he's not Anthony," his mom said through her tears. "You should come to the hospital right now."

"Of course, I'll be right there mom," Anthony said. Holding onto his phone, he leapt up from the bench, then ran along the pathway through the park back to his car. When he arrived at the hospital, he first saw his mom and his sister Maria. They were both very sad and crying. A few of his friends were also there, as was his wife Kelly. Although he was surprised to see her, the focus of his attention was on his father, who laid in the hospital bed covered with bandages on his upper body. As he walked into the room towards his father, he saw that he was also hooked up to an IV and that his eyes were closed. As he stood looking at him, wondering if he would be okay, his sister Maria rushed over to him and held onto him tightly, crying on his chest. Holding her, he looked over at his mom and asked, "What happened mom?"

He had never seen his mom look so devastated as she answered, "Someone ran a red light and hit him really bad."

Anthony felt horrible inside and, letting go of his sister, he walked over to his mom and hugged her. Then he asked her, "Can I have some time alone with dad, please?"

"Sure honey," she agreed, as she retrieved a kleenex from her purse and wiped her eyes. "We'll be in the waiting room." Everyone else took this as a prompt to allow Anthony to visit with his dad alone and walked out to the waiting room with his mom. After they had all left the room, Anthony walked over to the side of his dad's bed so he could be as close to him as possible. He wasn't sure if his dad was completely unconscious or not, but he started to talk to him anyways.

"Hi dad," Anthony said somberly. "I know you can hear me. I just wanted to tell you I'm sorry about yelling at you and saying those rotten things. I didn't mean any of it, I was just really angry. I want you to know that I love you so much, and I'm so thankful for everything you have done for our family."

After saying this, Anthony became choked up with grief and started to cry. He clenched his hands around the railings of his father's hospital bed, realizing how intensely he loved him. He felt like he had more to say to his dad, so after awhile he continued. "I don't know what's wrong with me dad, but I'm just not happy right now and I need your advice so bad. I hate my job. I can't even look at myself in the mirror anymore knowing what I'm doing to these people. You taught me so much better than this, and I let you down. But I want you to be the first to know that I'm quitting my job. I was hoping you could quit yours too, and we could open up a business together. What do you think?"

Anthony cried a little more, looking at his dad and feeling so bad that his dad couldn't say anything back to him. "I love you dad. And I'm so sorry about everything. Please make it through this, and I won't let you down again. I promise."

A minute later, the nurse walked into the room and told Anthony that visiting hours were over. She assured him that the best thing for his father to recover quickly would be plenty of rest, but that Anthony could come back the next day to visit him if he wanted.

"Okay," Anthony whispered to her. "Just give me one second, please." He leaned over the railing of the hospital bed and kissed his father on the forehead saying, "I love you dad." After this, Anthony walked out of the hospital room and into the waiting room where everyone was still sitting. He immediately noticed Kelly sitting off to the side looking out the hospital window to the sprawling parking lot in the sun. Although he felt nervous, Anthony approached her somewhat hesitantly and said, "Hi Kelly. Thank you for being here. It means a lot to all of us, especially me."

Kelly appeared unemotional as she looked at Anthony and said, "I didn't do it for you, Anthony."

"I know," Anthony said, feeling shards of guilt and silent torment inside him. "But I just wanted to say thank you." He looked down at the ground in disbelief that the woman he had loved so deeply was now so cold and distant from him. Although he knew he deserved it, that his actions had caused her to feel the way she did and to threaten to divorce him, he just couldn't make sense of it, and it all felt so wrong. "Kelly," he stammered. "I'm so so sorry about what I did. These last four
years I really lost touch with who I was, and I can't believe I hurt you so much. I love you more than anything in the world Kelly. And I really don't want to lose you."

For some unknown reason, hearing Anthony say all these things just made Kelly feel angry. Although she was deeply hurt by all that Anthony had done to her, what came out as they met like this was her anger. "If you love me," she accused him, "then how could you cheat on me with that slut!"

"I don't know Kelly," he said, feeling slimy and tortured inside. "But I can tell you one thing: I don't love her or have the feelings for her that I have for you." He paused a moment, and added, "I love you baby, you and no one else." Anthony was telling her the truth. Although, things were so badly fucked at this point that not even the truth made any sense. Indeed, the more tender and caring Anthony became, the more hostility Kelly displayed in reaction to him. After having been so monstrously betrayed, she was now utterly defensive and retaliatory.

After he told her he loved her, she lashed out at him, "That's a complete lie Anthony! You're totally full of shit!" She was so upset it was hard for her to speak, and her words came out choppy and distressed. "It's no wonder you're so good at your job," she continued, pushing through the emotional cracks in her voice. "All you do is lie. Maybe that's all you're good at! That's probably why I never know when you're telling the truth anymore."

Kelly looked away from him. Inside herself she thought about how she had decided to divorce him, about how she simply couldn't live with a man who had lied to her for so long, a man who had fucked another woman for long weekends while she waited faithfully at home for him. She felt incredulous that the man she loved and to whom she had been so completely devoted could cut her heart like this, could vilify their love behind her back. Thinking these thoughts only made her heart more bitter and her tongue more biting. "I've been there for you through thick and thin, even when you didn't have a god damn pot to piss in! Do you remember that? And now ..." Kelly had difficulty completing her thought or stretching the sentence any further, as it was, in fact, a death sentence. The death and the end of the love they had shared. The death of her dream of living with Anthony for the remainder of her life. "Now you repay me for my years of love and devotion by fucking some whore at your office?!?"

There was nothing Anthony could say to console her at this time. However, although some part of him knew it was over, he couldn't help but keep trying because, although his actions had been heinous, had been unforgivably and gruesomely injurious to his wife, deep down he was like a confused little boy who had spent his life grasping for whatever he wanted. Although he really did love her, perhaps he did not know how to love her the way that she needed to be loved. Perhaps he was just too damn needy for attention and sex from whatever beautiful woman might give it to him. Standing nearly speechless before his wife, Anthony felt the deep emptiness inside him, the emptiness he had been trying to fill with sex and drugs and workaholism. He knew that the only thing that had even come close to truly filling that empty void inside him had been Kelly. But he was eons away from her now.

"I'm sorry Kelly, you're right. But please just give me another chance," he pleaded. "I promise that I will never let you down again. Just one more chance honey, please!"

Kelly looked as if her heart had descended a thousand feet below her into the ground, through the roots of trees and the graves of souls, deep down where all was quiet and still and even the dead did not stir. Then she looked up at him and said, "I don't know if I can do that, Anthony. I just don't trust you anymore." These words filled him with the most horrible dread he had ever experienced. "I'm sorry, I have to go," she said. As she spoke these final words, Anthony could see a great upheaval of sadness rise inside her, and she began to cry as she walked quickly away from him and out of the waiting room, not saying goodbye to anyone.

THIRTY-THREE

ANTHONY WENT HOME THAT NIGHT and drank a few beers alone while sitting mindlessly in front of the TV. He felt his life collapsing. He would have called a friend, but he was in one of those dark psychological states that sometimes scare friends off. Anyways, he wouldn't know how to tell a friend what was going on inside him because it was too much, coming from so many angles of his life that he was overwhelmed and numb. So he decided just to wait it out. What was done was done, and though he had fucked things up real bad, all he could do now was try to make the best of it. Although his father was in a serious condition at the hospital, his prognosis was fair. The doctor had said that often times people who have been involved in car accidents like his father show a severe trauma reaction at first, but then recover well. He hoped what the doctor said was true. But that night—with his father in the hospital, his wife wanting to divorce him, and his job having led him to do things which he now realized had totally compromised his own integrity and self-respect— his entire life was in a state of chaotic disarray.

The next day, Anthony needed to escape his brooding thoughts and clear his mind, so he set out for a drive to the mountains in his new red Ferrari. After a few minutes, however, an unmarked car behind him flashed police lights, so he pulled over to the side of the road. *Jesus Christ*, Anthony thought to himself. *I thought things were already as fucking bad as they could get.* He watched in his rear view mirror as three men wearing suits exited the vehicle behind him and approached his car. The lead man came to Anthony's window and motioned for him to roll it down, while the other two stood at the front and back ends of the passenger side of his car. As Anthony rolled down his window, he said with both exhaustion and annoyance, "What the hell's going on?"

"Are you Anthony Cousto?" the man inquired in a serious and demanding tone.

"Yeah, what's going on?" Anthony asked, feeling more stressed.

"We're agents from the Economic Crimes Division, and we'd like to have some words with you. Can you please step out of your vehicle and come with us."

Anthony's heart pounded in his chest as he asked, "Am I being arrested?"

"No. Not at this time, but it would be in your best interest to come with us," the agent replied.

Anthony thought about it for a moment. He really didn't want to leave his Ferrari parked on the side of the road, but he was also very concerned about what the hell was going on. As usual, he was of the mindset to deal with it right away, and he didn't need another unanswered threat hovering over him; so he agreed.

"Alright, let's get this over with!" Anthony said. He got out of his car and followed the main agent to their unmarked police car with the other two agents trailing behind him. He got into the backseat, where one of the agents kept a close watch on him while they drove to a nearby police station. There, they ushered him into an interrogation room of sorts, and asked him to wait. A few minutes later, the main agent entered the room with a cup of coffee which he offered Anthony, and a very thick file in a manila folder which he dropped onto the metal table. The agent was tall and slim. He wore tinted reading glasses and had pale, chalky white skin that looked as if it might fry up quickly in the direct light of the sun.

Before the agent could say anything, Anthony, still with a strident attitude, asked, "So what the hell is all this about?"

The agent sat down at the table across from Anthony and said, "I'm going to make this really quick and easy for you Mr. Cousto. We've been conducting an investigation on Fairtex Mortgage for over a year now, and we have enough evidence to charge you along with several of your co-workers with fraud, among other things." The agent paused for a moment, opening up the folder and looking through it. "We know all about your late night magic sticking, as you call it. And we've decided to make you an offer since you have the most to lose."

"How do you figure that?" Anthony asked him bluntly.

"Well sir, since we have been conducting our investigation, you have perpetrated more fraud than anyone else in your office. This means you are looking at a lot of time," the agent said. "If you are found guilty of the crimes, and we do have a very strong case against you; you're looking at about ten years. However, we are willing to reduce your sentence if you are willing to help us get what we want."

Anthony felt a lump forming in his throat as he paused to consider what the agent had said. He was hoping that if he complied fully with them he could get off the hook for the whole thing. Thinking along these lines, he responded, "If I do help you, I don't wanna do any prison time."

The agent smiled sardonically and said, "That's not going to happen Mr. Cousto. Like I said before, with the evidence we have against you already you're looking at ten, maybe fifteen, years. There's just no way you're going to walk away from this without doing some time."

Anthony was suddenly filled with apprehension as he asked, "How much time are we talking about?"

"Maybe two years. But you'll be out in one," the agent said as if to reassure him.

"Shit," Anthony muttered in consternation. "I need some time to think about this."

"Well, you have until tomorrow Mr. Cousto." The agent handed Anthony his card and added with great severity, "Call me in the morning and let me know. Remember, I'm only offering you this deal once, and that's it."

Anthony sat back in the uncomfortable chair and shook his head in disbelief. He was once again amazed at how rapidly his life was going to hell. One day he had been riding high like a warrior in his glory, the next he had been cut down like a vagabond groveling in filth. All he had left was his home and his security, and now with the pending charges perhaps all of that was at risk too. Standing up to leave, he told the agent he'd think about his offer and was escorted back to his car. After revving up the audacious engine, he drove off into a whirlwind of confusion and calamity.

~ THIRTY-FOUR ~

ANTHONY SAT IN A LOUNGE CHAIR in his backyard at
twilight. He was holding a drink and enjoying the view of
the trees as they slowly changed color and darkened with
the setting sun. He needed to decide what he was going to
do about the deal the agent had offered him, but so much
had happened so fast and unexpectedly that he was completely perplexed. Fortunately, his mom had called during
the day to tell him that his father's condition was improv-
ing. He had wanted to go to the hospital to visit him, but
he'd been so shook up by the police that he was virtually
crawling inside his skin. So he'd decided the visit would
have to wait. Then, Angelina had called wanting to come
over. Although he really just needed to be alone to determine his own fate, he'd agreed, and she was on her way.

Sitting alone in the dim light, he thought very hard
and even prayed a little; although, his situation was so terrible that he didn't know if any amount of thinking would
even help. The prospect of going to prison for ten years
had seriously disturbed Anthony. He'd heard about big-
wigs getting busted for this kind of thing before, about
fraud and money laundering and Ponzi schemes, but he
didn't think his ridiculous magic sticking would ever get
him caught up with such grave consequences.

Sipping on his drink, Anthony flipped through the yellow pages looking for a reputable lawyer to contact. The lawyers all had cheesy smiles and complicated names that Anthony didn't even want to try to pronounce. At last he gave up, thinking that he himself knew he was guilty, so what use would trying to build a fabricated defense case be? He realized that he'd probably have to take the rap and be responsible for all his fuck-ups. Like his dad had told him a few times, "You've made your bed Anthony, now you've got to sleep in it." Although he had always disliked this saying, at the moment it rang true.

Deep in thought and considering the consequences of his actions, Anthony heard Angelina come into the house and walk through to the backyard. She came from behind him and put her hands around his chest, kissing him lightly on the neck. "Hi baby," she said softly. "How are you doing?"

"I'm okay I guess," he lied. He hadn't told her about his visit with the agents. He hadn't told anyone.

As Angelina walked around him to the outside bar to fix herself a drink, she asked him, "So why haven't you been to work?"

Anthony shifted a little restlessly in his chair and told her, "My dad got in a car accident and I've needed some time to think, that's all."

"Really?" Angelina said, surprised that Anthony hadn't told her before. She walked back over to him with her drink, and asked, "Is he going to be okay?"

"He'll be fine, I think."

"Why didn't you tell me before?" Angelina asked him. "I had no idea you were dealing with this."

"I wanted to, but I really just needed to be alone for a little bit 'cause I've been dealing with a lot of shit this week. Can you understand?"

"Yeah, of course," Angelina reassured him. However, she felt slightly put off by his not having told her and added, "but I would've at least liked to have known what was going on."

Feeling pressured, Anthony said with a bit of tension in his voice, "I'm sorry, okay?"

"It's okay. I understand," Angelina replied, sensing that he was very upset. Then she added playfully, "So what else have you been thinking about? Me, I hope."

"You know I have!" Anthony said smiling and feeling a bit lightened by her mood. Then, on a more dramatic note, he added, "Kelly filed for divorce."

"What?" Angelina was shocked that Kelly had filed so quickly. "Already? What the hell?"

"Yeah," Anthony concurred with her sentiment. "And she moved back home with her mom, too."

Angelina took this as a sign that maybe her relationship with Anthony could get a little more serious. "Does that mean you want me to move in now?" she asked him in an encouraging tone. Then, becoming aware of her supremely bad timing, she added, "Just kidding, baby."

Although Anthony enjoyed her playfulness and her humor, his mind was drawn to the very serious situation in which he was now embroiled. He looked at her square in the eye and said, "There's something else I wanna tell you." After pausing a moment, as if it was necessary for him to gather the inertia to speak, Anthony said, "I've decided to quit my job at Fairtex."

"What?" Angelina gasped. "Why?"

"Because I'm sick of it!" Anthony exclaimed. "And I'm tired of screwing people over." He paused to let the gravity of what he was saying sink in. Then he added, "I don't care about the money anymore. I talked to my dad and we're gonna open up a new business together."

"Really," Angelina guffawed. "What kind of business?"

"I don't know yet," Anthony said, feeling frustrated. "It doesn't matter, as long as it's not mortgage."

"Wow!" Angelina took a deep draw off her drink, and said, "I'm really shocked. You're making all this money and you just wanna throw it all away?"

"Yeah, actually I do," Anthony said resolutely. Then, paraphrasing what his father had told him, he added, "It's not all about money, baby."

Hearing this made Angelina feel angry and even a little resentful. "For me it is!" she quipped. "I don't wanna be poor,
Anthony. I like being able to do whatever I want and go wherever I want." Her face showed the strain of a rise in blood pressure as she became more flustered and added, "My parents were really poor, and I'm not about to go through what they did again. Not as an adult!"

It was amusing to Anthony how much Angelina sounded like he did about a week earlier. But after all that had occurred recently, his mind had been changed and he viewed things differently. However, he felt the disguised threat in Angelina's voice, so he asked her, "What are you saying? If I quit, you
don't want to be with me?"

"Yeah," Angelina affirmed his suspicion. "That's exactly what I'm saying." She paused to reflect about her future, and added, "Once I get married, I don't want to work anymore. And I want a man that's going to be able to provide me with all the things I need." She was coming to terms with her own priorities and trying to explain them to Anthony. "Let's face it," she continued, "starting your own business is really risky. And to be honest with you, I don't want to take any chances like that right now."

Anthony was dumbfounded by her response to him. He had thought she would be more supportive of his decision, but he also understood that she wasn't in the middle of the same crisis that he was. "I sure wasn't expecting that!" he exclaimed to her.

Angelina empathized with his pain and came over to comfort him and try to persuade him not to quit his job. "Anthony," she said, "I do love you. And I want to be with you. Can you please not do this and stay? We have such a good thing going right now, with the amount of money we're both making we can retire in five years." Looking at him with those same big, brown, sad eyes that she had first shown him in his office a couple of years ago, she implored him, "Is there anything I can do to change your mind, baby?"

Anthony slowly brushed Angelina's hands off of his body and stood up. He looked at her with sincerity, and said, "No, there's not. I've made up my mind Angelina. You're either with me or you're not."

Angelina looked down at the ground in pain. Then she stood up and looked at him with anguish in her eyes and said, "Sorry, I'm not." She picked up her purse and walked back through the house and out the front door. As Anthony heard her start her car and drive off, he leaned back in his chair once more and took another sip from his drink. He looked around him and realized that the chips were beginning to fall and that his life was going to take on a new shape, that some new order was beginning to form out of the chaos and destruction.

THIRTY-FIVE

THE NEXT DAY, Anthony went to work. He had already contacted the agent and had made up his mind what he was going to do. He walked directly to Mr. Blake's office and knocked on the door. Mr. Blake asked him to come in and, seeing that it was Anthony, exclaimed, "Hi Anthony! What's going on buddy?"

"Not much Mr. Blake," Anthony answered. Though it was hard for him to say what he had come to tell Mr. Blake, he continued. "I just wanted to thank you for everything you have done for me. And I wanted to let you know I have decided to leave the business."

Mr. Blake was very surprised to hear this. "I see," he replied. "Have you told David or Frankie about this yet?"

"No, Mr. Blake," Anthony answered with a sullen voice. "I wanted to tell you first, sir."

"Okay," Mr. Blake replied. Then he picked up his phone and dialed a number while saying, "Wait one second Anthony." Then he spoke into the phone, "David, can you please come into my office, and bring Frankie with you." He hung up the phone and said, "Anthony, I want David and Frankie here with us because you've caught me off guard with this. I definitely don't want you to make a decision until we all get down to what's bring-ing this on, if you don't mind."

"No, that's fine, sir," Anthony said, feeling both respect and admiration for Mr. Blake.

There was a knock at the door, and Mr. Blake told them to come in. As David and Frankie walked into the office, they looked a bit confused. Then David said, "What's up Anthony, how you doing?"

"I'm good, sir," Anthony replied.

The three of them were standing there awkwardly looking at each other, so Mr. Blake said, "Can everybody sit down please?" As everyone found a seat, Mr. Blake continued. "I'm sorry to say that Anthony just came by to tell me he wants to leave us."

Lister looked at Anthony with an acute expression of shock on his face and exclaimed, "Why? Bro, you're fuckin' killing it here! Are you stupid or something?"

Knowing that Lister had a predilection for being very intense, David chimed in, "Anthony, what Frankie is trying to say is you're our best loan officer and our top revenue producer. What can we do to change your mind?"

Anthony felt the pressure from his bosses, but he knew this was the moment of truth and he needed to come clean with them. "Can I be honest with you guys?" he said, more as a statement than a question.

"Yes, definitely!" David declared.

Anthony didn't know exactly where to start, so he opened his mouth and hoped the right words would come out. "I'm just really sick and tired of lying to my clients, over and over again, just to get their business."

Mr. Blake showed a look of concern on his face as he asked Anthony, "What type of lying are you talking about Anthony?"

"You know sir," Anthony explained. "The type where I promise the client one rate, and then at the signing they get one that's much higher. Not to mention, the fees are much more than my original quote too. It's just really getting to me now." Anthony felt himself becoming exasperated with how intensively he had been instructed to manipulate his clients. "And I'm sick of coming here at night and doing you know what."

"And what is that?" David asked him.

"I think you guys know exactly what I'm talking about!" Anthony exclaimed, on edge.

"No, we don't Anthony. Please tell us." David countered.

"Okay, things like changing people's paystubs, tax returns, and bank statements. All the dishonest bullshit we do just to get the loans approved. I'm tired of doing all that!"

"Bro," Lister spoke out hurriedly. "I told you before, you don't have to do that! Just let someone else do that for you."

"Wait a second now!" Mr. Blake spoke in a commanding voice. "I don't think anyone should be doing that in the first place. You understand Frankie." With that, he gave Lister a wary look. Then he continued, "However, Anthony, if your work load is too much to handle, then let some other people help you out." Mr. Blake's voice sounded more understanding as he said, "Now, I know that your father has recently been in a car accident, and I'm sorry about that. I hope he recovers quickly. I also know that a family crisis can put a lot of strain on a person and sometimes mess with your head. Maybe what you need is a nice vacation to get away and clear your mind of all these troubles."

Anthony felt guilty about his decision to leave Fairtex Mortgage. Mr. Blake had been nothing but kind and incredibly generous with him the whole time. That's why he struggled to try to tell him that he just couldn't continue working at Fairtex Mortgage. But all he could manage to say in response was, "I don't know, sir."

Mr. Blake looked at Anthony with a slightly puzzled expression, then said, "Why don't I send you to Cabo for a week you can even stay at my Villa it's right on the beach you'll love it? Everything will be paid for, and once you get back we can talk about this stuff again. How does that sound?"

"Thank you, sir," Anthony said. He realized that Mr. Blake was really concerned about him, and had his best interests in mind, but things were now beyond the point of repair. So Anthony told him, "I really do appreciate the offer Mr. Blake, but I just don't think it's going to change anything."

At this point, David interjected, "Hold up, Anthony; let me ask you something. You've been doing this for about four years now, right?"

"Yes, sir. About that," Anthony replied.

"Right. And you know that lying, or whatever you wanna call it, is part of every sales job in the world, right? You think lawyers don't lie, or dentists, or even doctors? Everyone does, Anthony. It's part of making money in this world." He paused a moment, then added, "You remember the first time I met you?"

"Yes, I do Mr. Konn." Anthony nearly smiled thinking back to that day.

"What did I tell you that this job is all about?"

"Making money."

"Right," David said. "And sometimes little white lies are what it takes to get the job done, because ninety-five percent of these homeowners are complete idiots." He looked at Lister and laughed, then added, "They don't know the difference between the rate they pay or their APR. Think of it this way Anthony, when you go to a dentist and he tells you that you need work done, you believe him right?

"Yeah," Anthony said. Even though he knew David was just wasting his breath trying to convince him to stay, he was polite enough to hear him out and not appear like a totally insane asshole.

"Did you know," David continued, "that a very high
percentage of dentists make their living off charging you for shit they don't even do?" Anthony nodded his head in agreement. "So you think all of them should quit? No, that's just part of the game. You're either playing or you're just sitting on the bench watching." Feeling like he was making some headway, David continued more emphatically. "Where do you want to be next year, or in five years, Anthony? Making thirty thousand dollars at some mediocre company, or making over a million a year like you are right now? That's what you have to ask yourself." David's speech had been both compelling and convincing, Anthony thought. It was a shame he was preaching to a hanged man who couldn't continue even if he wanted to.

Mr. Blake wrapped up the meeting by saying, "Anthony, here's what I want you to do. Go to Cabo and think about
everything we talked about. Then come back and tell me personally what you want to do. Now, before you go, I want you all to understand that none of this discussion we just had is to ever circulate around the office or to be spoken of to anyone else outside this company. And I personally never again want to talk about lying or changing documents or whatever else, ever. I don't want to hear about this bait and switch shit or what's going on in this office after hours again. Understood gentlemen?"

Anthony, David, and Lister all quickly replied, "Yes, sir." Then the three of them left the office and went their separate ways. While David and Lister returned to the frantically furious world of selling bogus loans to unsuspecting and naive customers, Anthony walked the other way, outside of the building and on to a nondescript building across the street. Entering the office he'd been instructed to report to, Anthony greeted the Economic Crimes agents and began to take off the wire he'd been wearing during his final meeting with Blake.

The agents smiled and congratulated Anthony on a job well done. Managing a dour smirk, Anthony sat down as the agents replayed the recording and told Anthony they had enough evidence now to indict Blake on criminal charges and launch a full-scale investigation of all his associates. Anthony felt sickened by the idea that his work colleagues would probably be convicted of the same crimes as he would. But, in the end, he felt had to protect himself, and doing two years was a whole lot better than ten to fifteen. And with his life in the utterly fucked up shape it had gotten to, Anthony thought a year or so spent in a place far from this world of worries and woe might just do him a little good.

As it turned out, Thomas Blake was sentenced to nine years and Al got four. David Konn and Frankie Lister both were handed down with five years. Ethan, Snowman and Tyson got off with probation. The judge went light on Anthony, as the agents had promised. As for Angelina, Anthony never learned of her fate in the ordeal, and he never heard from her again. Like a cyclonic dream, she had swept through his life recreating and destroying everything he had loved. And, now, she too was gone.

When it was all over, Anthony could only look at the entire situation as one big, reckless adventure that had taken him places he never knew he would go. From rags to riches to rags, and from love through lust to loneliness, all Anthony could understand was that forces greater than himself had impelled him, had taken hold of him and thrust him through a great series of bizarre events and experiences. Striking a deal with the authorities had been a good decision and would enable him the time to reflect on all that had transpired. Although it was not the ideal resolution to his wildly broken life, it provided an interruption to the deteriorating state of his spirit. And through facing the consequences of his past actions, Anthony would have the opportunity to reconsider the path his future life would take.

~ THIRTY-SIX ~

ANTHONY SERVED HIS TIME. Fifteen-and-a-half months to the day. Although the experience of temporarily losing his freedom was in some respects entirely hellish, all in all, by complying with their plea bargain, he'd struck a good deal with the prosecution and was released as a young man with most of his life still ahead of him. Sure, he'd screwed everything up on his first go round, but then again, it had been so easy to do! Anthony realized he was only human. After all, everyone just wanted to be rich and successful in America, right? Wasn't that the irresistible illusion Anthony had gotten caught up in to begin with?

The day he got out of prison, Anthony's dad was there to pick him up. He had recovered from his car accident while Anthony did his time and was pretty much back to normal when Anthony was released. Going to prison showed Anthony that some people would be there for him no matter how horrible his situation became, like his mom and his dad. It also taught him something about who his real friends were, because lots of the guys he hung out with when he was rollin' in the cash suddenly disappeared when he got into trouble and lost it all. Others, like Ethan, had shown their true colors by coming to visit him when he was locked up.

Once Anthony got out of prison, the mortgage industry had collapsed. Taxpayers had bailed out Wall Street—the very people who allowed all those quixotic loans to even exist—and no one had put any of them in prison. No one wanted to take the blame at the top, so it all just rolled like shit downhill onto the mortgage brokers. What they didn't tell you is that brokers don't approve loans. Wall Street does. Everyone knew what was going on, from the very top executives on down to the underwriters who approved the loans. But no one said a word because money made them all turn the other way.

Wall Street didn't care; as long as homeowners kept refinancing their homes, the greedy fucks could keep cashing in on the prepayment penalty and a year's worth of interest. They just wanted their millions of dollars in bonuses. The guidelines to obtain a residential loan were so easy that all anyone needed was a heart beat and a social security number. It was that easy. The reality is that Anthony didn't create no-documentation loans. Wall Street did. Brokers just used the tools they were given to close loans any way they could because no one ever verified anything.

In four years of working in mortgage, Anthony made a little over 3 million dollars until, because of greed, he lost it all: his wife, his house, all his cars, and all his hard-earned cash. But what really kept him up sleepless at night wasn't losing all his money or going to prison, it was the fact that majority of his clients had lost their homes because of the dishonest loans he gave them. He could never change that. And it would haunt him for the rest of his life.

ABOUT THE AUTHOR

Arsalan Saadati has worked in the mortgage industry since he graduated from Cal Poly in 2003 with a B.A. in business finance. He worked as a branch manager at one of the largest subprime lenders in America before becoming a mortgage broker. In 2006, Broker Banker magazine named him the "Top Rising Star" in the mortgage industry. *Loan Officers Wanted* is his first book of fiction.